Democratizing the Global Economy

The Battle Against the World Bank and the International Monetary Fund

Edited by Kevin Danaher

Common Courage Press
Monroe, ME
Philadelphia, PA

Cover design by Matt Wuerker and Erica Bjerning
Page layout by Kevin Danaher

Library of Congress Cataloging-in-Publication Data
Democratizing the Global Economy : The Battle against the World Bank and the IMF / edited by Kevin Danaher.
   p. cm.
  Includes index.
  ISBN 1-56751-209-7 (cloth) -- ISBN 1-56751-208-9 (pbk.)
  1. International economic relations. 2. World Bank. 3. International Monetary Fund. 4. Structural adjustment (Economic policy) 5. Economic assistance--Developing countries. 6. Democracy.
I. Danaher, Kevin, 1950- .
HF1359.D46 2000   332.152--dc21   00-064532

Common Courage Press
Box 702
Monroe, Maine 04951
Phone: (207) 525-0900
FAX: (207) 525-3068
www.commoncouragepress.com
email: orders-info@commoncouragepress.com

First Printing

Contents

A note about the cover from the publisher: Could America become a force for economic justice, as symbolized by the eagle chasing the global robber barons? It may seem a far-fetched dream given the U.S.'s ugly hand in globalizing the economy. Whether this dream becomes a reality depends largely on how many Americans join those protesting in Seattle, Washington, Prague, and elsewhere.

Acknowledgments

We would like to thank the individuals and organizations who so kindly allowed us to use their material in this book: AlterNet, Chapter 21; FAIR, the Media Watch Group, Chapter 3; 50 Years Is Enough Network, Chapters 4, 11, 14, and 24; *The Nation,* Chapter 20; *In These Times,* Chapters 2 and 16; *Multinational Monitor*, Chapters 9, 13, and 15; *ZNet*, Chapter 6.

My deepest gratitude to Miranda Ritterman, Sarah Norr, Priscilla Huang, Shawn Green, Tony LoPresti, Ingrid Mollard, Tiffany Page and Kristina Klein who helped with research, proof-reading, and the many other tasks involved in producing a book of this kind.

Special thanks Matt Wuerker for his artistic skills and cool politics, and to Arthur Stamoulis, Greg Bates, Laura Lefler, and all the other wonderful folks at Common Courage Press who, as always, were great to work with.

Thanks to Maya, Arlen and Medea for constant love and affection.

My deepest appreciation goes out to the tens of thousands of people who turned out on the streets of Washington, D.C. in April 2000 to send a message to the rulers of the planet that we are determined to have a democratic global economy, whether the rulers like it or not!

Introduction

Kevin Danaher

In April 1999, when the 50 Years Is Enough Network mobilized activists outside the spring meetings of the World Bank and International Monetary Fund in Washington, D.C. there were approximately twenty-five protesters. One year later, in April 2000, there were approximately 25,000 protesters. Clearly, something had changed.

A key turning point came on November 30, 1999 in Seattle when tens of thousands of protesters scuttled a crucial meeting of the World Trade Organization (WTO). When we saw the awesome potential of mass, nonviolent civil disobedience to disrupt meetings of the global elite, the word went out over cell phones and e-mail networks even before the tear gas had cleared in Seattle: "Come to Washington in April and we'll do to the World Bank and International Monetary Fund what we did to the global trade bureaucrats—give them a taste of participatory democracy."

World Bank/IMF officials tried to put the best face on events when tens of thousands of committed activists surrounded their Washington offices in mid-April. They tried to persuade the public that they—not the protesters—were the ones most concerned about ending poverty in the world. They heaped aspersions on the demonstrators, calling us names and asserting that the people in the streets didn't know what they were talking about. Yet a high percentage of the people in the streets possessed a detailed critique of World Bank/IMF policies. This grassroots, street analysis had been cultivated by a growing number of books, educational videos, professors, student groups, and organizations dedicated to exposing the record of these powerful institutions. The 50 Years Is Enough Network had grown from its original six groups in 1994 to more than 200 diverse organizations across the United States. Criticism of IMF/World Bank policies had been seeping into the mainstream media. Even Congress had gotten into the act by appointing a blue-ribbon panel (the Meltzer Commission) which, following a year of research, recommended significantly downsizing both institutions.

On the two main days of their April 2000 meetings, the bankers were not able to ignore our presence. They had to get out of their hotels by 5:00 A.M. in order to get to their conference rooms before we protesters blocked streets with our bodies beginning at 6:00 A.M. They needed thousands of police to facilitate meetings that traditionally required no more than a few rent-a-cops.

It is extremely telling that the bankers and their defenders in the corporate media shunned debating us. They avoided dealing with the substance of our critique and focused their energies on *ad hominem* attacks instead: We were dirty, ignorant, ill-informed, spoiled and shouldn't be listened to. Yet if we are so misinformed, it seems that the defenders of the status quo would rush to engage us in public debates so they could show us up for the know-nothings they accuse us of being. Quite the contrary! When the *Jim Lehrer News Hour* on PBS asked the movement and the IMF/World Bank to put up some debaters, the movement sent Juliette Beck of Global Exchange and noted Indian author Vandana Shiva. The Bank and IMF refused to have their spokesmen appear on the same evening, thus forcing the *News Hour* to have two nights, one for the bankers and one for us.

Let this stand as a public challenge: Any time and any place they are willing to face us in public debate—preferably on nationwide television—we will put up representatives of the movement and we will win the debate!

Another key reason for the movement's strength is the changing politics of the U.S. trade union movement. A mere two years earlier, the AFL-CIO leadership had supported the Clinton administration's request to Congress for an additional $18 billion for the IMF (a 50 percent increase in IMF resources). Now the AFL-CIO was openly allying itself with organizations calling for the abolition of the Bank and the IMF.

Another powerful component of the opposition movement is the role played by activists from the global south and the moral authority of the constituents they represent. The activists in the streets were bolstered by the sharp minds and voices of people such as Trevor Ngwane, a town councilor from Soweto, Walden Bello of Focus on the Global South in Thailand, Vandana Shiva of India, and many more. At 6:00 A.M. on the morning of April 14, two dozen activists from more than ten countries gathered in the street outside the posh Washington home of World Bank President James Wolfensohn. We held signs calling for debt cancellation and we sang songs from many lands—softly, so as not to wake the neighbors. When a phalanx of Washington, D.C. police came zooming up in cars and motorcycles, we convinced them that we wanted to do nothing more than present Wolfensohn with a letter from a number of global south organizations supporting a new campaign to boycott World Bank bonds. When Wolfensohn tried to go from his front door to his limousine and we surrounded him, he and his security people were visibly nervous. When he tried to snatch the statement and make a getaway, Dr. Vaneeta Gupta of India insisted he stand still and listen to her read the statement, so we would know that he heard our critique.

These and many other incidents filled the week of activities and filled participants with an empowering sense that we may actually be able to change the course of history. We dragged these institutions out into the glare of public opinion. We penetrated the corporate media with a critique of top-down globalization. We built feelings of trust and camaraderie among different sections of the movement. Veterans of the A16 events went back to their communities to organize locally around global issues.

The Washington protests were followed in late September by massive street demonstrations in Prague, Czech Republic, at the annual fall meetings of the IMF and World Bank. Though marred by violent confrontations on the streets and widespread brutality against arrestees by the Czech police, the Prague protests reinforced the message to the bankers that profit-making can no longer be the dominant priority for the planet.

The demonstrations in Prague were linked to local protests around the world on September 26—a Global Day of Action Against Corporate Rule. Some fifty U.S. cities and more than a dozen other countries saw protests against local manifestations of corporate rule.

The movement has grasped the value of this tactic of disrupting business-as-usual for the global elite. And most activists understand that mass mobilizations are just that—a tactic—to be used in combination with other tactics within a larger strategy of profoundly transforming the global economy.

Paradigm Shift

The movement for global justice that is putting increasing pressure on the rule-making institutions (World Bank, IMF, World Trade Organization) is laying the ideological and cultural foundations for a paradigm shift of historic proportions. In contrast to the money cycle that is the central organizing principle of the corporate elites, the movement is organized around the life cycle (human rights and protecting Mother Nature). Whereas the core values of the corporate paradigm focus on maximizing profit and increasing the quantity of things a person owns, we challengers focus our core values on the quality of relations among people and between people and the environment. The dominant paradigm emphasizes economic growth, and measures everything— whether clear-cutting forests or overfishing the oceans—as a positive number, measured by the annual percentage increase in the Gross National Product.

The challenging "life-cycle" paradigm is creating institutional building blocks for a sustainable global economy with no starving children; an economy that leaves the planet for future generations in better condition than it was when we received it.

We hope that you will use this book as a tool in building the movement for global democracy. We do not mean democracy in its traditionally narrow political sense (electing wealthy men who supposedly represent the rest of us in the halls of government). We mean democracy in the broader sense of citizen sovereignty: people *running their own lives* in all spheres (political, economic, cultural). Indeed, we believe that if humanity does not awaken soon from its political sleepwalking, we will be confronted with social and natural disasters that are currently unimaginable in the scope of their horror.

Democratizing the Global Economy

The title of this book refers to a general process taking place around the world. What does it mean to democratize the global economy? It means moving capital investment decision-making from the secret realm of the wealthy few out into the light of public control. The word democracy implies that sovereignty (ultimate political authority) resides in the people, not in the corporations. This powerful idea is now spreading around the world.

Democratization of the global economy is taking at least three forms. The first—dealt with in this book—deals with the institutions that make and enforce the rules of the global economy. By forcing these institutions to change their rules away from a focus on maximizing profits for private corporations toward meeting social needs and saving the environment, the mass movement is gradually democratizing institutions previously characterized by antidemocratic behavior.

The second section of the movement for democratizing the global economy focuses on corporate accountability. The trade unions, the anti-sweatshop movement, the environmental movement, progressive legislators, the socially responsible investing movement, and many more are forcing corporations to change their behavior. Companies under pressure often do little more than put out better propaganda, but they are realizing that the movement for corporate accountability cannot be ignored. As the November 6, 2000 issue of *Business Week* noted: "...it would be a grave mistake to dismiss the uproar witnessed in the past few years in Seattle, Washington, D.C., and Prague. ...they have helped to kick-start a profound rethinking about globalization...".

The third piece of the movement for planetary economic democracy does not know itself to be a movement yet. There are thousands of micro-enterprise lending groups, local currency organizations, cooperative business ventures, trade unions struggling to control their pension funds, community development schemes, and worker-controlled enterprises building a new, more democratic economy from the grassroots up. In addition, there are hundreds of groups experimenting with things such as community supported agriculture (CSA), which directly links farmers with families buying produce in order to cut out the market and the large corporations that dominate the food distribution system. All of these grassroots efforts are attempts to mitigate or eliminate the pernicious influence of the profit god. When these efforts get linked up—something many people in the movement are talking about these days—the impact will be huge.

Future books from Global Exchange will focus on the second and third aspects (corporate accountability and alternative economic institutions) of this global democratic revolution. This book focuses on the movement to change the rules of the global economy, with special emphasis on the World Bank and the International Monetary Fund.

The first section of the book ("The Art and Science of Protesting Transnational Elites") documents what actually happened in Washington, D.C. during the April 2000 protests outside the World Bank/IMF headquarters at their annual spring meetings. It is important to analyze critically how these events were organized and how the establishment responded because the 50 Years Is Enough Network and other organizations are now committed to mounting mass protests whenever the World Bank and IMF hold major meetings in Washington (e.g., October 2-4, 2001).

The second section of the book ("Why the World Bank and the IMF Suck") provides detailed analysis of the policies and the ideology of the World Bank and IMF. We encourage you to use the material in this section of the book to reach out to those of your fellow citizens who are not yet convinced that these institutions are part of the problem rather than part of the solution.

The third section of the book ("Where Does the Movement Go From Here?") includes articles on the state of the movement; tactics and strategy for democratizing the global economy; and alternative ways to organize economic activity so it gives priority to meeting social needs and saving the environment rather than to maximizing profits for corporations.

Creating a Values Revolution

At Global Exchange we work with grassroots activists all over the planet. There is definitely something happening. People are tired of elite politicians running their societies in the interests of the wealthy few. They are fed up with seeing their natural environment being treated as a commodity, to be sold to the highest corporate bidder. They sense the danger of their children being brainwashed by corporate commercialism into believing that life is about material acquisition rather than love and solidarity.

A growing number of people are challenging the cult of powerlessness: the widespread cynicism that we can't change reality, that "there is no alternative" and we are helpless to alter the course of events. A common expression of this sense of powerlessness is when people say "but I'm only one person, what can I do?" As if any one of us is more than one person!

In recent years, particularly among the youth, this cynicism (from the Greek *kynikos*, meaning "like a dog") has been losing its appeal. The social crisis and the environmental crisis are forcing more people every day to shift their worldview to a more activist perspective. More and more young people are learning to organize—something the university only teaches in business school—and they are turning their organizing skills toward the full democratization of global society.

Among the "best-and-brightest" in our society there are two groups: those who want to make tons of money and those who want to make history by saving the planet and humanity from destruction. I know which of these two groups I want as my friends.

If this book helps, in even a small way, to debunk the cult of powerlessness and wake people up to the need for a global values revolution—away from the money cycle toward the life cycle—then it will have been well worth the effort.

Straight from the Horse's Mouth

The plain truth is that market liberalization by itself does not lift all boats, and in some cases, it has caused severe damage. What's more, there's no point denying that multinationals have contributed to labor, environmental, and human-rights abuses.

The extremes of global capitalism are astonishing. While the economies of East Asia have achieved rapid growth, there has been little overall progress in much of the rest of the developing world. Income in Latin America grew by only 6% in the past two decades, when the continent was opening up. Average incomes in sub-Saharan Africa and the old Eastern bloc have actually contracted. The World Bank figures the number of people living on $1 a day increased, to 1.3 billion, over the past decade.

The downside of global capitalism is the disruption of whole societies. While the industrialized countries have enacted all sorts of worker and environmental safeguards since the turn of the century, the global economy is pretty much still in the robber-baron age. Yet if global capitalism's flaws aren't addressed, the backlash could grow more severe. Already, the momentum for new international free-trade deals has been stopped cold.

"Global Capitalism: Can It Be Made to Work Better,"
Business Week, Special Report, November 6, 2000

Section One:

The Art and Science of Protesting Transnational Elites

Because the April 2000 protests in Washington marked a historic turning point in the struggle against the World Bank and the IMF, this section deals with what exactly happened: how the protests were organized, how the events changed people's lives, how establishment institutions responded, and how the public discourse was transformed.

"Granny Goes to Washington, and Goes to Jail" is the very personal story of Margot Smith, whose life was transformed by becoming part of a global movement for change. She provides a unique, ground-level analysis that you will not find in textbooks.

Terry J. Allen's essay, "D.C. Police Broke the Law to Keep Order," documents the many ways in which the police violated our constitutionally guaranteed rights just so the bankers could hold their annual spring meetings.

In "For the Press, Magenta Hair and Nose Rings Defined Protests," Rachel Coen deconstructs the bias of the corporate media as they defend the status quo against our alternative worldview.

Njoki Njehu and Soren Ambrose ("How A16 Was Organized") give an insider account of how activists in Washington created what was—in the words of D.C. Police Chief Charles Ramsey—one of the best organized protests ever held in Washington.

"Lessons from Seattle and Washington, D.C." by author and

veteran nonviolence trainer Starhawk, presents important insights for future mass mobilizations.

Michael Albert ("Assessing A16") provides a political overview of the Mobilization for Global Justice, and suggests directions for future outreach and organizing.

Alli Starr's "The Power of the People" concludes Section One by reminding us of the many strengths of the movement, and by situating the current movement within the larger historical context of previous struggles.

1

Granny Goes to Washington, and Goes to Jail

Margot Smith

The twenty thousand demonstrators in Washington, D.C. who opposed the policies of the World Bank and IMF are good news for all of us who are concerned about our democracy and the condition of our planet. Most marchers were young people—high school and college students, people with young families. These activists are smart, knowledgeable, disciplined, and concerned about social issues. Many were willing to go to jail for their convictions. The issues they covered ranged from environmental damage by corporate hog farms in North Dakota, to saving the redwoods in California, to freeing Tibet. The next generation can and will carry on our fight.

I went to Washington because of my concern about the world-wide economic and social influence of these institutions that are not accountable to the public. My consciousness had been raised at the Beijing Women's Conference in 1995, where I met women who were victims of IMF "Structural Adjustment Programs": policies requiring countries to commit much of their gross national products to servicing their foreign debts. Because of their debt, these developing countries have to cut healthcare, education, and other social programs. Much of the brunt of IMF economic restructuring falls on women whose children are destined to be hungry, disease ridden, and illiterate, and who themselves are thrown into poverty and prostitution.

Before leaving for Washington, I knew that I wanted to be in an affinity group. I wanted to be involved in a group action. To this end, I attended WB/IMF planning sessions at Global Exchange, and was eventually invited to join Save the Redwoods/ Boycott the GAP, a group led by Mary Bull of San Francisco. I also went through training in nonviolent resistance run by the Midnight Special Law Collective. A friend of Mary's offered a house in Washington where we could all stay, and sixteen of us camped there for several days. Another granny and I were housed in a sun porch on the second floor and we were quite comfortable.

> *PRESS RELEASE: As the destruction of California's redwood forest continues to profit the billionaire Fisher family, owners of GAP, Inc., and as the GAP persists in using sweatshop labor, activists with a sense of humor will sing, dance, and strip off their clothes in protest, Saturday, April 15, at 2:00 P.M., at the GAP in Georgetown.*

Mary Bull is an artistic genius at street theater. At her home in San Francisco we made banners, costumes, and sashes. On April 15th we demonstrated in front of the GAP store in Georgetown. My role was video maker. About two thousand people were packed on the sidewalks in front of the GAP, where police lined up in force to make sure that we all stayed on the sidewalk and did not block traffic. The group performed a dance which showed cubes spelling out SAVE REDWOODS then BOY-COTT GAP, then STOP SWEATSHOPS, then chanted "We'd rather wear nothing than wear GAP" and stripped down to their underwear to great cheers. A picture of the strip-down was on the front page of the *Washington Post* the next day. In spite of elbow-to-elbow crowds, jostling, and police restrictions, a ten-minute video came out of the demonstration and has been sent off to Free Speech TV.

On Sunday, April 16 at 5:30 A.M. we arrived at Washington Square in downtown D.C. to assemble for action. Thousands were gathering from all over the world to register their dissatisfaction with the current economic model and to renew their commitment to creating an economy that fosters equity and justice, not just the bottom line.

A few of our group attended a spokesperson session the previous day and had agreed for us to be the No Compromise Flying Squadron, which meant that we were to provide diversions when needed, that is, when the police or others were in a tense or confrontational situation. The plan was that we were to receive instructions from designated messengers as to where we were to go and perform our chants and dances. We were all handed maps with D.C. segmented into sectors, and we were assigned to sectors A, B and C. Our messenger reported where we were to go, and we headed off to the barricades.

People congregated in groups at every corner, like ghosts appearing out of the mist. Suddenly, there were thousands of us and we spread throughout the downtown area and blocked off many streets. The weather turned bright, sunny, and warm.

The police used iron-barred barricades to close off ninety square blocks around the World Bank headquarters and did not allow us to get close. They closed two subway stations. Demonstrators, as they had done in Seattle, locked arms and blocked intersections for several blocks around the barricades. Some intersections were blocked off with human blockades and also with twine and yarn in creative weavings around lamp posts and traffic signals. Some protesters dragged barricades (large pipes, boxes, and trash containers) into the intersections.

We went from intersection to intersection, chanted and danced and watched other actions. Four of us were dressed as redwood trees with foam leafy headdresses and a brown foam trunk—I think that there are at least 1,000 pictures of me in my redwood costume; everyone with a camera seemed to click at us. "Hey Hey, Ho Ho, Corporate Greed has got to go. Spank the Bank. This is what democracy looks like, this is what democracy feels like..."

I Get Adopted

At one intersection, a young woman came up to me and said that her group had decided to adopt me as their grandma. I said, "Of course, I would like to meet you." So she took me over to a group of eighteen who had locked arms across the intersection. They were from North Dakota and were protesting the corporate hog farms that are ruining the environment. As Grandma, I told them that I was very proud of them and gave them all hugs.

On Sunday, for the most part, the police did not engage with our protesters but stood silently with crossed arms and billy clubs. However, there were instances when they used pepper spray and clubs, often in out of the way places where they were not observed by many.

Our cab drivers were from developing countries and very supportive of our efforts to close the World Bank. They personally knew of the devastation caused by their policies, perhaps they even immigrated because of them. One Pakistani driver told us that he had refused a fare to the World Bank.

The Sunday night spokesperson's meeting consensus was that on Monday everyone would march around the perimeter of the World Bank enclosure, ending up at the Ellipse. The aim was to educate the public rather than close down the meetings. Because many had to return home after the weekend, the total numbers were diminished somewhat. Yet spirit, puppetry, costumes, signs, and chants were as strong as ever.

Monday, April 17 was rainy and cold. By noon, we arrived at the blockade around the World Bank building and this was the place where we would be arrested. There were some negotiations with strategists representing the affinity groups, and negotiations with police. I was impressed with the skill of the negotiators in arriving at a consensus—Mary made sure that only strategists from affinity groups had a say, and excluded casual bystanders (there were many) from the proceedings. The final decision was that the police would open up three barricades and those who would risk arrest would cross the line. I decided that after all these years, I had nothing to lose and would be arrested (my first time). I gave all my identification, my camera, and papers to Carolyn, one of our group, to take back to the house.

When it was necessary to spread the word of the action through the crowd, Mary would call out "Repeat after me" and the crowd would yell "Repeat after me." Then she would call out the information and it would be yelled throughout the crowd.

Our view was that inside the IMF/World Bank buildings meetings were taking place that would impact millions of lives and the future of the planet, yet there were human and environmental interests that weren't being represented. As activists, we were surrogate voices for the voiceless—for environmental protection, for human rights and fair labor, for social justice and racial equality, for clean air and clean water, for indigenous sovereignty, and for true democracy. As delegates, we felt we had a right to go in and represent these important issues that were being neglected in the IMF/World Bank biannual meetings.

The Street Scene

A double line of police stood with masks and billy clubs behind the barricades, and when the protesters pressed close, the police surged forward and sprayed us with pepper spray. At this point, we all sat down, both to defuse the situation and make it more difficult for the police to move us around. Those who got pepper spray in their eyes were treated by medics in the crowd, who washed out their eyes with solution. It was obviously painful. I only had two spots of pepper spray on my glasses, so I was lucky, although I did inhale a minuscule amount that made me cough. It was enough to convince me that I was very lucky to have missed this experience. For this old lady, sitting down on the wet street for any length of time was not easy, and I found that I had to move around to keep going.

The negotiations resulted in a compromise by which we would cross over the police line toward the World Bank with locked arms in three rows of ten, with a ten-foot aisle between the groups of three. The spacing was to prevent injury or harm in the crush of the crowd.

Mary, taking the lead, crossed the line. Immediately, billy clubs began raining on her ribs and abdomen. (She would later be diagnosed with a fracture.) The police began a mass arrest, totalling thirteen hundred people. One hundred sixty of those arrested chose to spend a week in jail and maintain solidarity so that all would receive the same sentence, keep our anonymity, and have the same treatment.

As we passed over the line and were arrested, each person was escorted by a police officer to the door of a big yellow school bus where we waited in line to enter. It was raining. We were cold and our clothes were saturated. We waited outside the bus for about thirty minutes while the police located their cameras and took our pictures, handcuffed us with plastic cuffs behind our backs, searched us, and loaded us on the buses.

I believe I received special treatment because of my age—the handcuffs were loose enough for me to wriggle out. In fact, I waved a free hand out of the bus window to one of the reporters videotaping the event, which amused him greatly. The people who went limp were carried on the bus by the police and received rough treatment, they were dumped on the floor of the bus.

Some had been told to carry nail clippers, and one young woman managed to use them to free the handcuffs of most of the people on the bus by the time we arrived at the next stop, the District of Columbia intake facility. When we were found out, the police were very unhappy because the handcuffs had our numbers on them and since we refused to give our names, our photo and number was our only means of identification. The photos were so smeary it was amazing that anyone could be recognized.

Welcome to the D.C. Prison System

At the intake facility, about fifteen of us women were imprisoned together in a large holding cell. It held a bench, and the floor was warm. On intake, we had to put all our possessions into Property, that is, plastic bags with our identification on it. Again, we declined to give our names, and could only be identified with our pictures and our numbers.

Then our handcuffs were removed and replaced with plastic cuffs which bound our right hands to our left ankles—again, mine were so loose I could extricate my hand, which I did in a subtle way. When hobbling in these constraints, the women dubbed themselves Igor, as in the Phantom of the Opera.

While we were in the holding cell (about five hours), we were not offered any food and we had to call a matron to use the toilet. The police officers outside our bars were eating donuts and coffee that was a form of torture for us.

After about five hours we were put on a city bus and taken to the court house. The police warned us that treatment at the federal courthouse would be severe, since the police there were U.S. Marshals. When we arrived, the bus was too large to fit in the tunnel under the courthouse where we were to disembark, so we were transferred to another bus and driven under the courthouse. Then I was fingerprinted and assigned a number, Jane Doe T192.

The marshals were strict, would harbor no talking or comments, made all kinds of remarks about us, and in contrast to the D.C. police, were mostly white with a military culture and they ran the place like a boot camp. They barked out orders, and some prisoners were slammed against the wall if they did not obey quickly. The holding cells were much smaller, held six of us with room for only three to sit on a bench. Again, we did not receive any food, but by now our clothes were slowly drying.

About 1:00 A.M. I was called to go in front of the judge. Three of us at a time were called. A lawyer was appointed to represent me, but in compliance with our lawyer's instructions, I rejected his services. I was charged with two counts and fined $100, which I refused to pay. I also refused to give my name. I was then sent back to another small holding cell with three others, and we waited for the next step.

After several hours, our hands and feet were shackled (it was painful to walk) and we were bused to the D.C. jail, unshackled, and placed in another small holding cell. There was a double-decker bunk, and three of us lay down on the top and three of us on the bottom, and we tried to sleep. Another three tried to make themselves comfortable on the floor. After more hours, we were called for processing, which meant that we were given a bracelet with a name (Jane Doe, 283-916), we had our pictures taken, were fingerprinted, and were taken to a small cell with a matron, where we removed our clothes (except for underwear) and were issued a prison jumpsuit and a toilet kit, which consisted of a toothbrush, toothpaste, soap and douche and iodine medication, and modess pads.

Then we were taken to medical services for screening. I said that I had asthma, so a physician took me in, and with the nurse, closed the door and asked what this demonstration was all about. I explained that we were opposed to policies of the World Bank, the IMF, and their effect on developing countries. He was from a developing country, commented that a relative worked at the World Bank, "but not in that section", and supported our position. He kindly gave me an inhaler—we had a sympathizer!

Finally, we were taken to our cells, and at 10:00 A.M. we were given lunch, which consisted of salad, beans, canned vegetables and bread. I wolfed it down.

Most of us had our own cells, although a few were two to a cell. All the women demonstrators were kept in their own cell block. My cell had a double-decker bunk, a desk and stool, a toilet and washbasin. My pillow was a roll of toilet paper wrapped in a towel. The door to the cell was solid steel except for a slot about two feet tall and five inches wide where guards could peer in. It was difficult to talk to my neighbors because they could not hear me unless we were both by the door. There was no television, radio, books, or anything else. By the time I got to my cell, I was so exhausted I slept for a long time.

There were three others from our group—Mary Bull

(Dragonslayer), Joan (Defender) and Rosabel Roman (Pilar). We met regularly during our stay, and tried to plan publicity for the group. Mary was a fantastic leader, artistic in dreaming up street theater. Joan, a granny (age seventy-three), was dedicated to the environmental movement and had been arrested many times, and was particularly concerned to not give her real name as she had outstanding warrants from other states. She never lost an opportunity to educate about the issues. Rosabel was quiet and observing, and was a volunteer at a Bay Area radio station. She spoke Spanish and was of Nicaraguan descent. I am a retired public health researcher whose main issue is universal healthcare.

One day we called out our occupations from our cells up and down the corridors. Most were college students, but Little Blossom was an activist from a Catholic Workers group near Philadelphia; Tree was a retired college nurse, Jane Addams a former social worker, several were activists against the School of the Americas, while others were with United Students Against Sweat Shops. There was a contingent from an affinity group in Berkeley called the Floating Barnacles.

The D.C. prison is staffed mainly with African-Americans—the guards, the medics, the warden, and of course, most of the prisoners. We observed groups of new prisoners coming through when we were outside our cell block, and it was dismaying to see such large numbers of these strong young men being sent to jail.

The cell block was very noisy. The guards would call out to each other day and night and the sound would echo off the concrete walls. Then, every night from 7:00 P.M. to 12:00 A.M., music was played over the loud speaker throughout the prison.

At 4:30 A.M. the guards called out "Chow time, ladies" and breakfast was served. We staggered from our cells and lined up to get our trays, grateful for being fed at all after our long fast. The food was salty and typically institutional—hot cereal, mashed potatoes; we had oranges twice and a banana once, canned pineapple, canned peaches, bread, waffles once, and so on. The orange drink had no fruit juice—when we were awake enough to notice, we did not drink it. Typically I would eat at 4:30 A.M., save some food for later and go back to sleep. Lunch was at 10:00 A.M., yet on some days we were permitted to eat in the dining area. Dinner was at 7:00 P.M..

The Human Condition

Most of the females arrested were college age. There were five of us grannies and a few women were in their thirties and forties. Our colleagues wore dreadlocks, were pierced and tattooed, and many smoked (to my surprise). There were some interesting human situations. One of the first happened during our medical screening. A group of women with a problem addressed the guards. One of their members, Lisa, was transgender, and they wanted to make sure that she was housed in the women's prison. We of course stayed in solidarity with them. The guards were stunned; first off, they were not accustomed to the problem, and secondly, did not know how to handle solidarity. The first night Lisa was kept in the mental-health unit, but then on our insistence was housed with us. She said that she was fearful of jail treatment, and that the guards had taken her out of her cell and looked at her for about fifteen minutes.

Among our group was a nursing mother (whose two year old was at home); an anorexic, an asthmatic, many vegetarians, some vegans, and a few kosher women. We were told that if we had a special diet for medical reasons, it would be handled by the medical unit; if it was for "spiritual" reasons, we had to go through the chaplain. In any case, it would take three weeks for the kitchen to accommodate a special diet. The chaplain came by the first day—she was an older black woman who looked at us with an expression of incredulity—we were not her usual clientele. One woman had been inadvertently caught up in the arrests, was horrified to be there, but once there, got into solidarity. Several were upset because their families or friends were not supportive, and would not accept collect phone calls.

On the second day, lawyers from the Midnight Special Law

Collective (MSLC) and from the National Lawyers Guild visited us as a group. They explained that MSLC lawyers were not licensed to practice in D.C. and that they would rely on National Lawyers Guild for representation in court. This was to change later. They told us that we needed to have consensus on our plea bargain—mainly, our charges (felony, misdemeanor, or infraction), if we would accept a fine, and whether to maintain anonymity. There were eight people charged with felonies which they would handle separately. They were in negotiation with the D.C. District Attorney and the Feds.

Group Process

The consensus model was used for our affinity group meetings, for meetings of our spokespersons, for strategy meetings, and in jail when we had to agree on our plea bargain. Everyone seemed to know the rules—I felt like I had been dropped from another planet. Here was a disciplined group process for effective decision-making that I had never heard of or experienced.

First of all, when voting, one "twinkled", that is, waved the fingers of both hands. During the discussion, one could raise a hand to make a proposal, express a concern, or ask a question. If things became complicated, we prioritized. When an issue was voted on, one could agree (twinkle), stand aside, that is, oppose the decision but not block action, or one could block the action. A special signal indicated "We love you, but please shut up."

A different facilitator was chosen for each meeting to protect people from being identified as a leader. Several were trained facilitators. A person designated as the "Stack," would recognize people when they raised their hands and stack them in order. Another was designated note-taker.

The advantage of consensus is that agreement is reached by everyone, and everyone has input. A disadvantage is that it takes a long time.

The prison guards, the warden, and other staff were fascinated by the group process and came to watch. Our meetings were held in the mornings and afternoons when we were allowed in the central dining area. We were also allowed to make collect phone calls, and I called home, called our Berkeley newspapers, and called my local friend Al Roat, who tried valiantly to visit us. Our local paper had a nice article, "Activist, 69, Released From Jail." The point, of course, was to keep the issues alive.

We decided to allow MSLC to negotiate for an infraction, which turned out to be jaywalking with a $5 fine. We held to the necessity for anonymity because several of us were from other countries and could be deported, and others had outstanding warrants in other states and could be imprisoned. They finally said we must give "a name." (One used "Malvina Reynolds.")

Because we were fearful that those in danger would be targeted, we wanted to have the power to select the order that we were to be released. We asked each person to state whether she was high, middle, or low priority, and a list was made up that mixed the three categories so that no one could be targeted. As it turned out, it didn't make any difference; they used their own order for whatever reason. We did suffer some anxiety, however, because one of our people who was most vulnerable had a delay, but in the end it was only because of inefficiency, not malice.

Our lawyer from the MSLC was Katya Komisaruk, a dynamic, savvy leader well-versed in civil disobedience. (She had led the training in Berkeley on Civil Disobedience after returning from four months in Seattle). One of the college women in jail had been accepted at U.C. Berkeley's Boalt Law School, and had taken a year's deferment because she wasn't sure she wanted to be a (corporate) lawyer. But after seeing Katya at work, she said YES. She was inspired. I was thrilled to see it.

The lawyers told us that a vigil was being kept in front of the jail, with between fifty to one hundred fifty people camping there in support. They were also risking arrest. When we would find out news from the lawyers or others, we would spread the news by calling out "Repeat after me" and shout phrases down the corridors.

April 20 was Passover. Subsahara, a college-age woman, asked the guards if we could have a Seder. We soon received word that the Jewish community was ready, the Catholic Chaplain was out purchasing food, and that there would be a Seder that evening. Everyone signed up to attend. It was held in the basketball court, and we all sat around the edges, leaning against the concrete walls. The Freedom Seder was led by Rabbi Deborah of Jews for Global Justice, and we shared matzoh, green celery, bitter horseradish, and the *charoset* (an apple, nut, raisin, and wine mixture), and drank grape juice on cue. It was a joyous celebration. We sang *Let My People Go, By the Waters of Babylon, Gonna Lay Down My Sword and Shield, Go Tell it on the Mountain, This Little Light of Mine,* and *We Shall Overcome.* Most moving were the young women who stepped in to lead the songs and rituals. They knew the songs well and were called on to represent their religion; a first for them to do so in a prison setting, I'm sure. Freedom had greater meaning for us all.

Creativity

One woman took cardboard from Modess boxes and made playing cards, then Jane Addams and Tree dealt hearts. Others took iodine from the douche kits and decorated their tee shirts with their names, hearts, numbers, and sayings. Others simulated tattoos with the iodine. One woman made jewelry out of Styrofoam cups, and several used their brassieres to tie their hair back. Several women from Florida led us in Radical Cheer Leading (Fat and Fabulous), and others made up a song:

"Have you ever been to the D.C. Jail
  at the very, very bottom of the justice system?
There you'll find quite a few resisters,
  who go by the name of Jane.
If you do, that's us,
We're Jane Doe.
We crossed the line, got pepper sprayed
  and now we're in cell thirty-nine,

Solidarity. It's working."

When we sang the song, a guard pretended to "conduct" it from the glassed-in guardhouse.

Our presence in jail caused hardships for other prisoners, which concerned us. Adding one hundred fifty prisoners to the system strained staff and facilities. Regular prisoners were used to do "detail" work, mopping, cleaning, and so on.

One day a young black woman pleaded with us to give our names and leave because the rest of the prisoners were on lock-down and could not leave their cells. They needed to call their children and families who "did not know if they were dead or alive. We've learned to be strong. I did a crime, now I'm doing time. Please finish your stuff and get out of here." Bertholt Brecht could not have written her words more poignantly. We explained that we would be gone in a day or so.

The guards were humane, except that they were guards. We needed socialization into correct prison behavior—occasionally they would say, "You cannot do that, ladies, you are in jail."

The prison system was anxious to be rid of us; we were expensive and straining the resources of personnel who had to work overtime. One judge thought he could be rid of us by calling us to court, appointing an attorney, and having us waive bail. He had the bad luck to get Mary (Dragonslayer) and three other very strong women in the first batch. When called, they stripped nude (noodling) and refused to go. The guards dressed them, and dragged them to court, where they refused legal counsel and refused to waive bail. That was the end of that idea. Unfortunately, Mary's wrists were injured when she was dragged by handcuffs.

A few of us were sitting around talking the last day and some mentioned that their allergies seemed to be better. We noted that the walls and floors were concrete and the mattresses were encased in plastic so there were few dust mites. The air was filtered and there were no growing things to release pollen and the food was simple—no chocolate, coffee, spices, and little cheese or eggs. It was a different kind of spa.

The prison system was very disorganized and inefficient. For example, we were fingerprinted with ink and pad when we first came into the jail (some systems use a scanner). Later, they took us to be fingerprinted again. Then, just before we were to be released, they wanted to fingerprint us again. Fortunately the warden intervened so we could be released sooner. She personally took over the release process in order to speed it up. She handed out our clothes and property, and by the end of the day, she was saying, "Repeat after me." We only saw two computers in the whole place, and judging from the signs posted around the jail, the literacy level of the staff was rather low.

On Friday night we were called down to a concrete hallway and there we sat and lay on the floor from 6:00 P.M. until we were released, in my case, at 2:30 A.M. Saturday morning. When we exited to the street, we were greeted with shouts and hugs, there was a van with hot soup and blankets, and we were asked to fill out forms describing any police brutality we had observed or experienced. I called a friend, Al Roat, who picked up three of our group and took us to the house in Mt. Pleasant.

The next day I went to the airport, where I had to exchange my ticket. The agent was a young African-American woman, and I explained to her that I had missed my plane because I was in jail for demonstrating. She asked "Why?" and I said, "Well, the rich are getting richer and the poor are getting poorer, and the World Bank and IMF have policies that help the process along." She said, "I think I can figure a way that you won't have to pay the $75 fee for changing your ticket." And she did.

I was glad to get home!

Now I am much more sensitive to the corporate takeover of the basics in our society and across the planet. Our movement for universal healthcare is really in opposition to the corporate takeover of the healthcare system.

The international and national media mergers, corporate farming, mining and forestry, housing development, gun control and arms sales, and even our universities and schools are all parts of the total picture. We *must* stand up for the environment, for women, for indigenous people, against racism and ageism, for labor, and for the common good!

What is Deglobalization?
Walden Bello

I am not talking about withdrawing from the international economy. I am speaking about reorienting our economies from production for export to production for the local market; about drawing most of our financial resources for development from within rather than becoming dependent on foreign investment and foreign financial markets; about carrying out the long-postponed measures of income redistribution and land redistribution to create a vibrant internal market that would be the anchor of the economy; about de-emphasizing growth and maximizing equity in order to radically reduce environmental disequilibrium; about not leaving strategic economic decisions to the market but making them subject to democratic choice; about subjecting the private sector and the state to constant monitoring by civil society; about creating a new production and exchange complex that includes community cooperatives, private enterprises, and state enterprises, and excludes TNCs; about enshrining the principle of subsidiarity in economic life by encouraging production of goods to take place at the community and national level if it can be done so at reasonable cost in order to preserve community.

We are talking, moreover, about a strategy that consciously subordinates the logic of the market, the pursuit of cost efficiency to the values of security, equity, and social solidarity. We are speaking, in short, about re-embedding the economy in society, rather than having society driven by the economy.

2

D.C. Police Broke the Law to Keep Order

Terry J. Allen

It's a win-win for everybody," said Police Chief Charles Ramsey, assessing the IMF/World Bank protests that rocked Washington in mid-April 2000. "The Bank was able to meet. The protesters were able to express their views and exercise their First Amendment rights, and we were able to maintain peace. We were able to keep ourselves from being the issue. That's a very thin line to walk."

Far too thin, charge some, for the legions of armor-clad D.C. police, FBI, Secret Service, and U.S. Marshals, National Guard troops, as well as neighboring law enforcement agencies that backed them up. As activists and lawyers review police conduct, they are uncovering a pattern of preemptive raids, restrictions, harassments, arrests, seizures, and instances of police brutality.

There is much to dissect: Police strategy was sometimes restrained and justified, sometimes technically legal but chilling, sometimes violent and disproportionate, and sometimes—civil rights lawyers charge—illegal and unconstitutional. Specifically, police violated activists' First, Fourth and Fourteenth Amendment rights, by restricting their free speech and due process, says Katya Komisaruk of the Midnight Special Law Collective, a mobile legal team that supports nonviolent activists.

John Sellers of the Ruckus Society, which trains activists in nonviolent civil disobedience, calls police tactics in Washington "far more insidious than in Seattle." In trying, as Ramsey put it, "to save the city," law enforcement agents surveyed activists, infiltrated meetings disguised as participants, conducted a mass arrest of more than 600 nonviolent marchers and bystanders, mistreated people in custody, confiscated First Amendment-protected literature, violated a contract with protesters' lawyers, and used the fire department (thereby obviating the need for a warrant) to search and then shut down the organizing headquarters. In violation of department policy, police frequently failed to wear identifying badges or give their shield numbers when asked; they failed to warn peaceful crowds to disperse before initiating arrests; and, they may have interfered with the phone lines of lawyers handling arrests. In the weeks leading up to A16, police prepared extensively, leaving little to chance. They spent more than $1 million on riot gear and high tech equipment and trained some 1,500 officers in crowd control using footage of Seattle. (Police also showed the video to area business leaders.)

During the demonstrations police maintained the upper hand, aided by good leadership, disciplined troops, helicopter, rooftop and on-the-ground surveillance, and informers. Robert Scully, executive director of the National Association of Police Organizations said that "Ramsey, and probably working with some of the federal agencies in D.C., was successful in infiltrating some of the groups ... and had firsthand, inside information of who, when, why, and where things were going to happen." Executive Assistant Chief Terrance Gainer says that, to his knowledge, no electronic surveillance was conducted since that would have required a court order and none was sought.

Many activists, however, cited numerous incidents of probable e-mail and cell phone interception. Lawyers bringing suit against the police say legal precedent, much of which dates back to the civil rights era, is on their side. They are also looking at cases such as *Collins v. Jordan*, a 1997 ruling by the Ninth Circuit Court of Appeals. It states that "the law is clear that First Amendment activity may not be banned simply because prior similar activity led to or involved instances of violence.... The proper response to potential and actual violence is for the government to ensure an adequate police presence and to arrest those who actually engage in such conduct, rather than to suppress legitimate First Amendment conduct as a prophylactic measure."

Ramsey, all but admitted to APBNews.com, a crime news Web site, that his actions were indeed prophylactic: "There were groups trying to agitate, and another group who could have committed acts of violence and vandalism. We wanted to neutralize these groups. No one wanted to see another Seattle."

Although the level of violence was far lower than in Seattle, brute force in Washington was never more than a nightstick away. Police insistence that their use of chemical weapons and batons was minimal and appropriate is countered by numerous observers. While Darth Vader clad cops sometimes ceded streets to demonstrators and ignored provocative actions, at other times they cracked down hard on nonviolent protesters or in response to minor infractions. Witnesses stood aghast when officers dragged a protester out of a crowd and beat him bloody or occasionally doused unresisting activists with pepper spray. Some demonstrators ended up in the hospital with broken bones and other injuries. AP photographer Heesoon Yim was hospitalized for a concussion and scalp wound after being clubbed. Ramsey defends the professionalism of his troops and says he has "No regrets."

The activists who came to Washington in the thousands were not without resources and planning of their own. In the week leading up to the April 16 and 17 mass demonstrations, they assembled from around the country and the world at the Florida Avenue Convergence Center. There, they analyzed the impact of the IMF and World Bank and received nonviolence training, street medicine and law, and media relations. In the grubby, chaotically energetic warehouse, an amorphous group of activists coordinated hundreds of media tours and prepared puppets, plans, pamphlets and thousands of meals.

Although police had roamed freely through the center for days;

surveyed the neighborhood, conspicuously writing down license plate numbers, and occasionally stopped and frisked people, they took no action until Saturday, the day courts are closed, the day before the main demonstration. "Once the Fire Department knew about the danger," said Gainer, "it had to act." Asked if police had given the Fire Department a heads-up about possible violations, Gainer answered, "The police and Fire did have ongoing conversations about that, yes." At 8:00 A.M. Saturday, with two fire inspectors in the lead, police rousted 300 groggy activists into the gray drizzle and sealed off the building along with medical supplies and tens of thousands of pamphlets on globalization, nonviolence and a host of other topics. They cited fire code violations and their "obligation to protect the kids." The prize capture of the raid was what police dubbed "a potential Molotov cocktail," a plastic bottle with a rag nearby, and no "accelerant."

In a triumph of the force of law over the power of reason, police also raided the Center kitchen where they cited chili, onions, garlic and gazpacho as "potential homemade chemical weapons." Two people were arrested. "What are they going to charge them with?" quipped Mara Verheyden-Hilliard of the Partnership for Civil Justice, a public interest law firm, "Unlawful possession of gazpacho?"

No one believed that fire code violations were the real reason for the closing, especially in a neighborhood where low-income renters plead in vain for attention from fire inspectors. But under this pretext, police were able to enter, search and close down the headquarters without a warrant. Gainer also said, "It was to our delight that it did discombobulate a bit the protesters and to the extent it threw them off balance, that was helpful too."

The admission that police closed the Convergence Center to disrupt the demonstration is corroborated by the department's subsequent refusal to allow protesters to retrieve medical supplies, literature and banners—a refusal that is central to one set of legal actions against the D.C. police. In a dramatic Saturday night maneuver, the Partnership for Civil Justice, a Washington,

D.C.-based public interest law firm, tried to force the city to release the materials. They got federal district court judge Thomas Hogan to agree to a Sunday 8:00 A.M. emergency hearing. Rather than see the issue come before the court, the D.C. Office of Corporation Council signed a contract agreeing to allow protesters to retrieve "First Amendment protected materials and medical supplies" and instructed "police and/or fire officials" to assist. "This will occur on [Sunday], April 16, 2000 at 7:00 A.M." in time for the Sunday demonstrations. "So, I get up there at 7:00 A.M.," says Carl Messineo of the Partnership of Civil Justice, "and this sergeant marshal says, this is his scene and he refuses to acknowledge the signed agreement and says nothing will be moved out. After multiple phone calls, he tells me with Orwellian logic he will honor the agreement but 'You will have to break in and if you do, I will arrest all of you for breaking and entering.'"

Gainer maintains that police really wanted to release the medical and other materials. "They couldn't get in," he said, since someone had broken off a key in the lock of the interior door to where the goods were stored. But the fact that it was police who secured the building raises questions: Was the inside door actually locked? Who locked it and when? And why did police forcibly open the outside doors around 10:00 A.M.. Sunday morning, while refusing to breech the allegedly locked inside door? "I have no idea how that happened," Gainer said. In a sworn affidavit, however, a locksmith called to the scene on Saturday afternoon to secure the outside doors said that all the interior doors, including the one to the medical room, were open when he arrived at 4:00 P.M. Saturday. They were open when he returned and toured the site at 7:30 A.M. Monday. The only reasonable conclusion you can draw," said Messineo, "is that police absolutely intended to restrict First Amendment rights." When police released the material Monday night—after the demonstrations ended—"My heart sank as a civil rights lawyer when I saw boxes and boxes of literature," he said. "They set out to make sure these demonstrators' political views would not be heard."

Some of the rumors that police spread were more inflamma-
tory than the alleged fire hazard at the Convergence Center. Gainer
told media that on Friday night, when police raided a Kalorama
Street house used by activists, they found "small caliber ammunition" along with the chains and PVC pipe. Three were arrested
and charged with possessing "implements of criminal intent."
Asked about the ammunition, Gainer said it was "a very, very
few." According to a woman staying at the raided house, the only
"ammunition" was fake bullets in her decorative cowboy belt
which police confiscated. Police records, said public information officer Anthony O'Leary, show no ammunition logged into
evidence from the raid. But the specter of violent protesters—
armed with Molotov cocktails and possibly guns—readied an
already nervous public for the whack of batons and whiff of pepper spray that was soon to follow.

Another preemptive police raid on several vehicles on
Wednesday netted seven people and PVC pipe (which could be
used to lock people down during sit-ins) and other "instrumen-
talities of crime." These raids, said Gainer, were implemented to
prevent the crime of impeding traffic. On the contrary, National
Lawyers Guild member Zack Wolfe said, "The point of these
preemptive actions was to frighten people and send the message
that if they participate in free speech activity, police will bust
down their door in the middle of the night and close down areas
where people are gathering to learn. There is no way it can't
have a huge chill on First Amendment rights."

The right to legal counsel may also have taken a hit. According to Komisaruk, telephones at the Midnight Special Law Collective were so tied up by heavy-breather hang-ups on Friday
and Saturday that people seeking legal aid could not get through.
As soon as lawyers tracked a call to the Institute for Police Sci-
ences and phoned to complain, the harassing calls stopped.

The message that protesting could be dangerous to your health
and freedom was sharpened on Saturday afternoon. After rally-
ing briefly at the Justice Department, a group of 1,000 people

marched a dozen blocks toward the IMF protesting the "prison-industrial complex." They were about to get a taste of the system they were decrying. Suddenly the police escort, which had been rerouting traffic in front of the march, and herding the demonstrators onto the sidewalk when they veered into the street, blocked the way. The marchers, not wanting a confrontation decided to disperse, but found their retreat was blocked by lines of riot-gear clad officers, who refused to allow either protesters or reporters to leave. Gainer, who was in the command center at the time, said that a warning to disperse had been given but he is "not certain who gave it."

Neither I nor any of the dozens of people I talked on the scene heard any such order. Hemmed in for 90 minutes on 20th Street by more than 200 police on foot and horseback, the protesters waited anxiously. Black armored personnel carriers and empty busses stood at the ready. The protesters, in the words of one speaker, were "intelligent, disciplined, and militant." They were also impeccably peaceful ... and scared.

That fear was fed by more than memories of Seattle. "We live in a country in which the Rodney King beating was determined to be appropriate police procedure, in which Amadou Diallo was shot 41 times," said Christopher Simpson, professor of Communication at American University. "What we see here, applied on a mass scale, is the velvet glove that covers the iron fist of police power that brought down Diallo." Fear levels rose when police ordered journalists to leave or face arrest. Most left but about 15 refused, because they thought their presence might mitigate or prevent extreme actions by police. "I have been covering this stuff for 15 years," said a trapped NBC cameraman, "and I've never seen anything like this."

In the end, announcing that the charge was "parading without a permit," police arrested more than 600 people. "You can't just arrest everyone," said Wolfe. "People have the right to be part of an assembly and to receive information." Police acknowledged that some of those caught up in the sweep were tourists in the wrong place at the wrong time or bystanders simply interested in hearing what the protesters had to say. One *Washington Post* photographer was also arrested. The mass arrests further "chilled dissent and kept crowds down for Sunday's mass demonstrations," said Wolfe, by instilling fear of being swept up in arbitrary arrests. They sent the message that "If you are in the vicinity when free speech happens, you are in danger of being arrested, tear gassed and hit with clubs."

While Sunday was relatively peaceful, the pattern of intimidation and selective arrests picked up on Monday, the day targeted by organizers for the most militant actions and mass arrests. Again, police seized the initiative, on one occasion swooping down and arresting a group of about 15 people walking down the K Street sidewalk. Dressed like Black Bloc anarchists, they were neither blocking pedestrians nor demonstrating and—aside from lowering the fashion tone usually set by "Gucci Gulf" three-piece lawyers and lobbyists—appeared to be committing no offense. A police search netted gas masks, "Seattle solution" antidote to chemical weapons, a box of nails and one slingshot.

Further down the street, another five young people lay spread-eagle on the sidewalk. After searches, some were arrested, some told to go on their way. The demonstrations came to a wet end that Monday afternoon with a wave of ritualized arrests when some 400 demonstrators offered themselves up to police. Some of those willing to risk arrest wanted to challenge the police more directly and break through the barricades. But with many of the more radical elements rejecting arrest altogether or already swept off the streets in preemptive police raids, those in favor of more ceremonial civil disobedience prevailed. As police orchestrated the pace, the cold, rain-soaked protesters walked slowly, row by row through an opened police barrier a few blocks from the IMF.

The arrests came after surreal negotiations between Gainer, holding a bunch of roses, and spokesperson Mary Bull, dressed like a molting tree. As one of his "concessions," Gainer agreed that the police would don their badges. By then, says Komisaruk, who would have preferred a more "robust" ending, activists were "chilled [both physically and psychologically], fatigued, and too polite." "Somebody whose sense of tactics was at one extreme, foisted her views on the rest of group," she said.

But activists' compliance on the street turned to resolute defiance and solidarity once inside Washington's jails. Many of those arrested reported that, out of the glare of cameras, police beat, intimidated and humiliated activists. Despite police preparations for thousands of arrests, numerous people reported that they were left in unheated spaces in wet clothes without blankets; some were not fed for 24 hours, others went long periods without water, some, despite nonviolence, were shackled ankle to opposite wrist, others endured homophobic and racist comments. Two people were taken to the hospital. Despite the abuse, 156 maintained solidarity until Friday, refusing to give their names until lawyers negotiated a plea bargain. Under the agreement, those in jail, as well as more than 300 already released who had not paid a fine, had their charges downgraded to jaywalking, with a $5 fine. Chief Ramsey was right that both sides won something. The D.C. police prevented "another Seattle" and gained accolades from media and colleagues, including police observers from Los Angeles and Philadelphia, sites for the Democratic and Republican presidential conventions.

The demonstrators turned downtown Washington into a militant, celebratory, anti-corporate free zone. They continued to expose the effect of the IMF and World Bank policies on the world's poor, the global environment and U.S. workers. The planned lawsuits said Verheyden-Hilliard "will seek to remedy the abuses and instruct police and national leaders that they cannot stifle dissent." "The fact that police used tactics usually reserved for armed terrorists is a testament to the threat that our movement represents," said John Sellers of the Ruckus Society. "That threat is the challenge we make to corporate power and the light we shine on such secretive institutions as the World Bank and IMF."

3

For the Press, Magenta Hair and Nose Rings Defined Protests

Rachel Coen

The success of the Washington, D.C. demonstrations against the IMF and the World Bank can be measured in part by how well activists communicated their message to the general public. Without a doubt, the Mobilization for Global Justice succeeded in intensifying the national debate on globalization. Mainstream media featured a more sustained and substantive discussion of World Bank/IMF structural adjustment policies than ever before.

That said, serious investigations of World Bank/IMF policies were still the exception rather than the rule. What's more, this small broadening of coverage was accompanied by a formidable backlash on op-ed pages, and by a rash of reports more interested in tittering at activists' fashion sense than in examining their politics.

One commendable investigation of the issues raised by World Bank/IMF protesters was Eric Pooley's *Time* article "IMF: Dr. Death?" (4/24/00), which analyzed how the World Bank and IMF have affected Tanzania, concluding that their policies "have hammered the poor." Also noteworthy was a front-page *Washington Post* article about Haiti by Michael Dobbs (4/13/00), which took a critical look at the suffering caused by the gap between the IMF's "free-market theory and Haitian reality."

On the same day, in what appeared to be an attempt at balance, *The Washington Post* also featured on its front page an article by John Burgess, "At IMF Headquarters, Embattled Staffers Wonder, 'Why Us?'" Celebrating the altruism of IMF staffers, the article joined them in wondering whether critics "understand the basics of how the Bank and poverty alleviation work." The article also painted a glowing portrait of World Bank president James F. Wolfensohn, who is quoted as saying that he is "doing God's work."

Individuals at the World Bank and IMF may well be principled, pleasant people. But is this relevant to an evaluation of the effectiveness of the Bank and IMF as institutions? Where Dobbs examined data about structural adjustment's impact on Haiti, Burgess focused on the emotions of IMF employees. These two articles illustrate a trend in the *Post*'s coverage of the issues raised by the protests—solid journalism on real world effects of IMF/World Bank policies was often "balanced" by uncritical reportage of the IMF/World Bank perspective, or by cheap shots at protesters' expertise and sincerity.

"Unwashed ... dazed"

For example, the *Post* ran an article on April 16 on the G-77's endorsement of the protests; most other outlets ignored this major story, and even the *Post* consigned it to page A31. On the front page that day was the article "Demonstrators Are United by Zeal for 'Global Justice,'" which purported to examine the politics of the Mobilization, but instead inaccurately concluded that the protest was "a demonstration without demands." It noted activists' "body odor," and reminded readers that "the fad factor cannot be denied. To have been in Seattle is to have reached a higher state of cool." Imagine, if you can, a *Post* news article making similar remarks about the way the IMF's Wolfensohn smells, or the "fad factor" behind the IMF's claim that it helps the poor.

One of the most striking reports in this genre was a National

Public Radio report by Guy Raz (4/10/00), which opened with the sentence, "Rule one for a warrior in the fight against global-ization: Take on a cool *nom de guerre* like. . .Mango." It went on to describe activists as "unwashed and somewhat slightly dazed." Raz's tactic of interviewing Jane or Joe (or better yet, Mango) Protester and identifying his or her views as representative of what is, in fact, a complex global movement was common throughout mainstream coverage. References to hair color, body-piercing and clothing were frequent.

It was in the op-ed pages, however, that the backlash was strongest. *The New York Times* was remarkable for its entirely one-sided op-ed page, which ran five pieces critical of the Mobi-lization and none that supported it or even treated its concerns respectfully. World Bank/IMF critics were not allowed to speak for themselves, but instead had their analyses caricatured by hos-tile commentators. In one op-ed (4/19/00), David Frum dismissed protesters as incoherent people who "hate dams and airports and economists." On the same day, *Times* foreign affairs columnist Thomas L. Friedman angrily declared World Bank/IMF critics to be "contemptible. . .economic quacks" who deserve to be given "the back of your hand."

The Washington Post did better at balancing its op-eds, run-ning four pieces critical of anti-World Bank/IMF activists, three supportive of them and one somewhat equivocal. Op-ed writers who opposed the protests, however, were given about twice as much space in the *Post* as those who supported them (3,780 words total versus 1,825 words). And as was true in other outlets, there seemed to be a lower quality bar for writing that opposed the protests than for writing that supported them. Witness Michael Kelly's "Imitation Activism" (4/19/00), a venomous tirade against the "tens of thousands of magenta-haired nose-ringers" whom Kelly accused of being "stupid" imitators of 1960s activism. "Actually, kids, not to be rude about it," wrote Kelly, "but it must by now have occurred to the swifter among you that you don't possess anything that can coherently be called a cause."

This refusal to take World Bank/IMF critics seriously was also evident in articles not explicitly labeled opinion pieces. Strangest was *The Washington Post* "Style" section profile of Ruckus Society program director Han Shan (4/15/00), in which reporter Ann Gerhart admonished: "Please do not call Han Shan a hunka hunk of burning radical love. That would be trivializing him." It is difficult, however, not to come away with the impression that Gerhart delighted in trivializing Shan—she pointed out that his shirt "cleverly matches his eyes," suggested that his "great looks" were a "recruiting tool" for his cause, and noted with evident surprise that "he neither sounds nor acts like a lunatic."

Unsurprisingly, a Nexis search of major media for the month of April found no articles in which IMF or World Bank officials were referred to as "hunka hunk" of burning anything.

People's Media Excluded

The many journalists who were refused admission to the World Bank/IMF meetings in April 2000 received a message from the IMF Press Office stating that the IMF does not accredit "public access TV, community radio, nor student or academic publications." The crucial category here is Community radio—the major source of daily news that does not have a corporate filter. It is indefensible for the IMF to deny access to community radio given that radio is the primary source of news in many of the developing countries that IMF/World Bank policy impacts most directly. This exclusionary policy marginalizes those outlets that are most likely to view the IMF's proceedings with a critical eye.

The IMF's e-mail address is publicaffairs@imf.org.

Support FAIR (Fairness and Accuracy in Reporting) by subscribing to their bimonthly magazine, *Extra!* Check their website: www.fair.org or call (800) 847-3993.

4

How the A16 Protests
Were Organized

Njoki Njoroge Njehu and Soren Ambrose

Where did it all begin? There are probably many who could claim to have thought of having large demonstrations at the Spring 2000 IMF/World Bank meetings. The 50 Years Is Enough Network, of course, routinely sponsors demonstrations at both the spring and fall general meetings in Washington, although the spring demonstrations are usually quite small (25-50 people). The November 30, 1999 protest in Seattle outside the WTO conference, in which thousands of activists put themselves on the line for global justice, inspired many to focus on April in Washington.

The first step toward making something big happen in April was to get a sense of what folks in D.C. were prepared to do. On December 15th, 50 Years Is Enough sponsored a "report-back" on Seattle at the University of the District of Columbia, which drew over 50 area activists. We capped the evening with a discussion of what could be done to build on the momentum from Seattle. The people present were enthused about the prospect of a big action in Washington in April.

On January 11, 2000, 50 Years Is Enough sponsored the first meeting expressly dedicated to planning the April actions. Over 70 activists showed up. Working groups were formed, a nonviolence agreement based on the one used in Seattle was agreed to, and the ball was rolling for the April action—dubbed 'A16' for April 16, the first of two days of meetings at World Bank/IMF headquarters.

Over the next several weeks, the group met and continued to grow, reaching about 120 at some meetings. Adopting a flexible consensus-based approach, employing working groups and a representative "spokescouncil," we built an atmosphere of mutual trust, and created the plans for what we chose to call the Mobilization for Global Justice. That name was applied to both our burgeoning coalition and the ten days of activities planned for April 8-17.

The Mobilization brought together hundreds of activists in Washington with an amazing array of talents and unstoppable dedication. Dozens of organizations and individual activists submerged their egos for the sake of creating quality actions and, almost as important, a microcosmic world of genuine solidarity and cooperation.

To draw lessons from the April events that may be useful for future protests, we give details below on the 16 Working Groups which worked together to organize the week of events.

Messaging: The first order of business was drafting a call for endorsements that was used, not only to garner support, but to simply inform people around the world of the Mobilization's existence and plans. The Working Group's focus then shifted to the composition and production of a four-page fold-out brochure offering basic facts about the IMF and World Bank and the week of actions in April. Also produced were a series of factsheets on such topics as the parallels between structural adjustment and domestic economic policies devastating the impoverished in the U.S. ("Adjusting America") and a history of organizing and major actions against the IMF and World Bank in the global South over the last 20 years. These factsheets are still available on the 50 Years website (www.50years.org). This Working Group also created designs for Mobilization T-shirts, stickers and buttons.

Arts in Action: This group provided the beautiful and festive puppets and other props that make actions like those in Seattle and Washington so visually impressive and which put on display the kind of world the movement for global economic justice is working toward: one with humor, beauty and cooperation. A body of people proficient in the art of making these props has been building over the last several years, including several in Washington, who were joined by others from around the continent as the action drew closer.

Communications: The Communications Working Group took on two main tasks: maintaining the website (www.a16.org) and co-ordinating the communications devices (cell phones, two-way radios, etc.) used by affinity groups during the direct action. The website was an especially valuable resource: it promoted the action around the world, recruited endorsers and participants, educated people about the IMF and World Bank, helped people find housing, carried a calendar of events not only for Washington but for related events around the world, supplied links to other relevant organizations and events, listed endorsing organizations, and provided space for dialogue. This group set up e-mail listserves for activists as they made plans for April. Many of the other working groups set up their own listserves to facilitate their work.

Convergence/Training: A series of nonviolence trainings, which introduced participants to techniques for protesting, blockading, and dealing with the authorities, were offered to Washington activists in the months leading up to April 16, and on a nearly-daily basis for activists arriving from out-of-town as the appointed days grew nearer. Trainings were also offered in how to deal with the media and how to facilitate meetings using a consensus approach. This group also took responsibility for locating the building used for the Mobilization's "convergence center:" the place used for most of the trainings, spokescouncils, prop construction, legal preparations, food preparation and provisioning. Located in a warehouse in the Columbia Heights neighborhood, the Convergence Center became the nerve center of the Mobilization. On the morning of April 15, the day before the actions, the municipal authorities went on the offensive and closed the center, confiscating most of the materials inside, on the grounds of alleged violations of the fire code. This harassment tactic failed to sideline preparations for the following day, as activists quickly regrouped at two nearby churches.

Fund-raising: The Mobilization cost over $140,000 when all was said and done, so the value of this Working Group should be obvious. About half the money was raised from small donations in response to a solicitation by the Alliance for Global Justice. Additional funds came from small foundation grants and some of the larger endorsing organizations.

Issues Forums: The Mobilization organized educational workshops about the IMF and World Bank starting April 10. In addition to daily sessions on the basic facts of the institutions and structural adjustment, there were also workshops on more specific topics such as the campaign for reparations for damages caused by Bank-financed large dam projects, bilateral investment treaties, and the campaign to boycott World Bank bonds. There was also a video series presented at the University of the District of Columbia and a local Jewish Community Center. The most popular event was a debate pitting Njoki Njehu, Director of the 50 Years Is Enough Network and Walden Bello of Focus on the Global South against representatives of the IMF and World Bank on April 15 at the Jewish Community Center. The debate drew hundreds of people, of whom only a fraction could fit in the venue—the largest we could find.

Labor: Labor was the only constituency to have a working group dedicated to it, due to the unique demands of dealing with union bureaucracies, and the potential significance of having major backing from the unions. And it succeeded: not only the AFL-

CIO itself, but a range of unions from the Teamsters to the Steelworkers to the United Electrical Workers (UE) and the American Federation of Government Employees (AFGE) lent their support to the permitted rally. The UE and AFGE also endorsed the Mobilization. By demonstrating that the coalition that came together in Seattle was united in opposing IMF/World Bank policies, we succeeded in getting our message heard by hundreds of thousands of people. We are now building on the relationship established with Jobs with Justice, and we look forward to collaborating on future aactions at IMF/World Bank meetings.

Legal: Teams of volunteer lawyers and paralegals associated with the National Lawyers Guild and Midnight Special Law Collective provided trainings for legal observers who sought to witness any actions by the authorities that might infringe on activists' rights. The legal teams provided trainings and advice for protesters who were risking arrest, and representation for those put in jail. Over 1200 people were arrested during the course of the Mobilization. Jail solidarity tactics succeeded in reducing most charges to the equivalent of jaywalking (a traffic offense) and a $5 fine—though that required several nights in jail under conditions some found abusive or intimidating. The legal teams continued working after the demonstrations to represent those whose charges led to court dates (in several cases the charges were dropped), and a lawsuit is seeking damages for police mistreatment, and spurious arrests and confiscations.

Logistics: Among the least glamorous but most-appreciated tasks was that of finding housing, parking, and food for the thousands of activists coming into Washington. Months of cajoling, lobbying, nagging, and pleading yielded thousands of places on area residents' floors and sofas, in tents in backyards and farms, and in churches and offices and union halls. The food was easier: Seeds of Peace provided mobile kitchens and supplies, which, together with donated food, allowed them to feed hundreds of people every day that the Convergence Center was open.

Media: For progressive activists in the United States, a key challenge has been to attract mainstream media coverage. In the wake of Seattle, our situation turned out to be different. Our debut press conference, immediately following a speech by World Bank President James Wolfensohn at the National Press Club on March 14, drew an overflow crowd of 60 journalists. Even before that, *Reuters* and the *Washington Post* had published stories on our plans. The Media Working Group fielded press calls and worked with reporters, securing particularly good coverage in, among other outlets, *Time* magazine, the BBC, CNN, and NBC. The Mobilization was, in the end, covered thoroughly by nearly every major media outlet.

Alternative and progressive media also covered the Mobilization extensively, with *The Nation*, for instance, printing a special issue on the week of events. The Independent Media Center was, as the name indicates, separate from the Mobilization for Global Justice, though it did receive a start-up grant for facilities and equipment from us. Its volunteers cooperated on many occasions with the Media Working Group, and with virtually everyone working for the media.

Medical: Our experience from the protests in Seattle convinced us of the importance of medical teams. Fortunately we had the help of several doctors and nurses with experience from Seattle and other actions. While there was less police tear gas to deal with in Washington, there was some pepper spray, and of course injuries from assaults by police officers with clubs, fists, horses, and motor vehicles. Many people also found themselves overcome by afternoon heat. The police complicated the medical effort by confiscating the majority of our first aid supplies during their raid on the Convergence Center.

Outreach: One of the central tasks in creating a successful action is getting people there. The Outreach Working Group, which focused almost exclusively on the Washington area, coordinated teach-ins and meetings with community groups, churches, and campuses to tell people why activists would be converging on Washington, and to encourage them to join the fun. The Mobilization hired a full-time staffperson to spread the message about the Mobilization to communities of color. A local crisis added urgency to the outreach effort as the city of Washington condemned several buildings, occupied mainly by immigrants, located in the same neighborhood as the convergence center—an area ripe for gentrification. The Mobilization took up the cause along with immigrants rights activists in the city, comparing the moves of the city government to the impact of structural adjustment on housing availability in Southern countries. The outcry from many quarters forced the city to delay the slated evictions, raise a $250,000 renovation fund from the building owners, and transfer ownership to the city—a major victory for the tenants!

Permitted Rally: Although many of the organizers were veterans of many a rally and march, few had planned an event as large as the one we organized for 20,000 people on the Ellipse, the park behind the White House. A quick learning curve was called for as the group negotiated for rally and march permits and good prices on sound and stage equipment, and learned the finer points of constructing a stage to National Park Service specifications. More negotiations concerned the appearance of many prominent speakers, such as heads of labor unions and various people's organizations from the North and South. In the end, the effort was a great success: lots of entertainment, stirring words, prominent speakers, and press coverage. The crowd was huge, and the short march over to the vicinity of the World Bank/IMF meetings allowed people to display their numbers, their message, and their support for all the forces opposing the IMF, the World Bank, and corporate globalization.

Roadshow/Caravan: Modeled on similar efforts made in advance of the Seattle WTO meeting, a troupe of musicians, improvisational actors, and activists was assembled and sent on a tour of campuses and cities up and down the East Coast, from Quebec to Florida, starting six weeks before the April actions. In their performances they provided introductions to the IMF and World Bank and urged audience members to come to Washington for the demonstrations. This Working Group also helped coordinate caravans of activists coming to Washington from all over North America.

Scenario: Charged with coming up with plans for the direct actions on April 16 and 17, this group had one of the most sensitive jobs. It gathered information on the likely movements of delegates and the police response, and created plans for street blockades to prevent delegates from reaching the meeting site at IMF headquarters. All plans formulated by the Scenario Working Group were submitted to the Action Spokescouncil, consisting of representatives of each affinity group participating in the direct action, which started meeting April 8. The ultimate outcome of this process was an agreement by affinity groups to take responsibility for specific "pie slices" of urban territory for the blockades. Although many delegates got up in the middle of the night to beat the blockades, which went up around 6:00 A.M. on the 16th, once these human barriers were in place, the authorities faced a difficult task in getting delegates through them.

Welcome Center: One of the last-formed Working Groups was a crew dedicated to making sure that the activists arriving at the Convergence Center would actually find people who could answer their questions and that journalists covering the activities there would not get in the way of vital preparations.

5

Lessons from Seattle
and Washington, D.C.

Starhawk

Just as we are able to organize internationally, so are the police. And just as we are drawing lessons from the last year of action, so will they. Unfortunately, I think we can expect them to learn the wrong lessons from the WTO protests in Seattle and the IMF/World Bank protests in Washington, D.C.

In Seattle the police essentially ran amuck. They not only shot teargas and pepper-spray at us, they also teargassed whole neighborhoods of the city, rounded up and arrested people who weren't even part of the demonstration, and were still ineffective (probably their worst sin) in keeping the windows of downtown Seattle intact or making sure the WTO meeting could go on.

Why were they unprepared for a blockade that was planned in open meetings for months ahead? My theory is that our style of organizing appeared to be so chaotic and was so different from what they define as 'organized,' that they just didn't see us as a threat.

Both the Seattle and D.C. blockades were organized in a decentralized fashion, with affinity groups who could make autonomous decisions on the street. Affinity groups sent representatives to a larger spokescouncil before the action to coordinate what we were doing and to make larger decisions. We also had Tactical and Communications working groups who came up with the basic scenario to surround the Convention Center, to have affinity groups commit to a certain "pie slice" of the map to defend, and to have "flying squads" who could move freely as needed.

This looked, sounded and felt chaotic while it was being organized, but in practice it worked beautifully. We had thousands of trained activists on the streets who knew just what they were supposed to do, and they had the flexibility to make decisions and change plans on the spot to respond to what was happening.

From the police point of view, it was disastrous. They came off looking both brutal and impotent. The city of Seattle was outraged, human rights advocates condemned them, and other police departments wondered how they could screw up so badly and let a few ragged demonstrators run them around.

In D.C. the police were more subtle and better prepared. The "police" in D.C. include dozens of different police departments, from the Park Police to the Secret Service, but they all share an attitude: "Hey, we're from D.C., we deal with demonstrations all the time. No way you scare us!"

In fact, we did scare them to the point that they essentially turned much of D.C. into a police state, blocking off 60 square blocks on A16 and 90 square blocks on A17. By then they had grasped the fact that we are actually extremely well organized, and that worried them. They were also extremely freaked out by the "anarchist costume"—black with ski mask or bandanna (simple, practical, elegant and slenderizing!)—and they seemed to think that any measures were justified in "saving the city" from this invasion of dangerous "terrorists."

They adopted the following strategies:

Surveillance: They read listserves and perused all the anarchist websites, undoubtedly tapped phones and infiltrated meetings, and probably used informants.

Pre-emptive strikes and illegal arrests: On Saturday A15 they arrested 600 people at a peaceful march, surrounded them, ordered them to disperse and then prevented them from dispersing. That morning they closed down the Convergence Center, just as thousands of new people were arriving to be oriented and trained. They confiscated the giant puppets, our medical supplies, and lots of peoples' personal property. Both these actions were illegal. We did get the puppets back before the demonstration, but not the medical supplies. Police Chief Ramsay was quoted as saying the raid on the Convergence Center had "discombobulated" the protestors. In reality, we regrouped quickly and still managed to train thousands of people that day, although I ended up doing one training in an alley. The police also raided a private home and stopped cars, confiscating lockboxes and other blockading equipment.

Propaganda and paranoia: The more the police can portray us as terrorists, the more they look like saviors and the more fancy equipment they can buy with beefed up budgets. So they claimed to have found a "Molotov cocktail" in the Convergence Center (our painting supplies), vats of homemade pepper-spray (the soup for our lunch), etc.

Relatively restrained and localized use of force: The police did use tear gas, pepper spray and did beat people in D.C., but mostly in smaller, more localized areas. They did not do vast sweeps through neighborhoods as in Seattle or attack the general population. Nor did they attempt to clear us all off the streets. Their general strategy was to set up their own barriers, establish their area of control, and then wait us out.

Negotiation: At one crucial moment on A17, Chief Ramsay came down and negotiated a voluntary arrest scenario instead of bringing out the tear gas and nightsticks. He's received a lot of credit for this, although in the light of all the repressive police actions, I can't quite see him as a great defender of democracy, especially given the brutal treatment the arrestees received in jail.

The truth is, none of these strategies could have stopped a single window from being broken in D.C. if that is what people had wanted to do. But Chief Ramsay was heralded as having "saved the city," presumably from acts of unspeakable terrorism. The police forces around the U.S. and worldwide are going to be studying these two actions in preparation for upcoming events—and most likely drawing the wrong conclusions: that surveillance, pre-emptive strikes and illegal roundups are the way to go.

What We Can Expect and What We Can Do

Surveillance: Assume that the police are reading the listserves. (Hello, police—I hope you at least are getting paid to delete 57 messages a day about a protest in Thailand.) Assume your phones are tapped, and that anything planned in an open, public meeting is known. Classic nonviolent theory accepts this, and says, "Hey, we're proud of what we're doing, we're not afraid of the consequences, and we have nothing to hide." I personally believe that most large actions are best organized around this philosophy, for a whole number of reasons, surveillance being only one. But if you do want to organize something that depends on surprise, don't do it on the internet, on the phone, or in an open meeting.

Pre-emptive arrests and disruption of our gatherings and meeting places: It may not be illegal yet to be an anarchist, but it may soon become extremely difficult to walk around freely if you look like one. I'm not suggesting you change your clothes or hairstyle—you have an absolute right to look however you want to look. But take extra precautions if you need to and do some careful strategizing about your visibility.

We also need to have backup plans of available spaces for trainings and gatherings. I know it's sometimes hard enough to find one space, let alone alternatives, but we should know what churches or union halls or schools might take us in in an emergency. That's what saved us in D.C.: A church and community meeting hall welcomed us in within hours of the police seizing the Convergence Center. We might also consider having several different puppet assembly sites, for example; and not keeping all the medical equipment, blockading aids or other vital supplies in the same place.

Police overresponse: The Jubilee 2000 folks, the trade unions, and the Mothers Against Drunk Drivers may still be able to have a big march without police interference, but I think we can assume that anything that looks like a direct action on the Seattle or D.C. or Mayday model may call forth the nightsticks and tear gas with very little provocation. Again, we simply need to be prepared and alert. If you bring children to a demonstration or have health concerns around tear gas, stay especially alert and keep an eye out for an escape route. Have someone prepared to do support for people who unexpectedly get arrested. Know who you can call for emergency help or to mobilize legal support.

Negotiation: Whether or not we negotiate with the police, and to what extent, is a political decision. The wisdom of negotiation may vary from action to action, city to city, moment to moment. We should bear in mind that some police forces may embrace negotiation, and we should be prepared to negotiate as one of our options.

Our Strengths

One purpose of nonviolent direct action is to make the inherent violence of the system visible. Every time the police overreact or arrest us illegally, we have in some measure succeeded. We have many strengths in this movement that we can build on to resist police strategies and violence. Some of them are:

The affinity group model: I don't envy the forces of repression; they have the daunting challenge of trying to stop a movement based on autonomous affinity groups instead of centralized leadership. It's a bit like trying to clear Bermuda grass out of the garden—remove one clump and the others just send out runners and spread. The affinity group/spokescouncil process gives us just enough coordination to be effective while leaving room for great flexibility, spontaneity and creativity in responding to the situation of the moment. The decentralized model of decision making provides an experience of empowerment that can be life-changing. Affinity groups also give us moral, emotional and practical support in an action. And they make it harder for infiltrators and provocateurs to operate. While we're forming affinity groups for these actions, we can build on their strengths by encouraging people to think of them as ongoing groups that might develop areas of special strengths and interests.

Trainings: The nonviolent direct action trainings make a big difference in how well people stand up to repression. Besides doing them just before an action, we need to develop more networks of trainers and find ways to offer them on an ongoing basis, so people can arrive for an action already prepared. This would also make them harder to disrupt by closing down a centralized space, as happened in D.C. More ongoing training would also help people better face police overreaction in local demonstrations. I'm personally interested in working on this.

Dialogue, consensus and diversity: All of us who have been activists for a long time have seen movements factionalize and splinter. During the recent actions, however, I've seen issues that could have resulted in schisms instead become something to discuss. I've seen a real commitment in people across the spectrum to dialogue about our differences and work out conflicts—even in the midst of the action itself. If we can continue in this mode, we might be able to avoid some of the mistakes of the past, and we will make it harder for the police to divide us.

Consensus does not mean unanimous agreement. It means we create a forum where all voices can be heard and we can think creatively rather than dualistically about how to reconcile our different needs and visions. If you want a more militant action and I want to bring my infant—how do we make that work?—rather than who is right and who is wrong. We need more ongoing forums for discussion. In the heat of preparation for an action it's hard to sit down and have a philosophical discussion about what nonviolence really means, or what economic vision we support in place of globalization, or whether property damage is appropriate. At least some of these discussions need to take place face to face, not just on-line, where we can actually see and hear the person behind the position.

Courage and commitment: I've been thrilled and moved to

see this incredible uprising of people willing to take risks, put themselves on the line, face violence and repression, and not give up.

As a middle-aged activist, I'm especially joyful to see so many younger people with such dedication and determination. So many of my generation gave up. If you don't, if you become lifelong activists, then it won't matter what the police do or don't do, we will change the world!

A tide of corporate high-mindedness seems to be sweeping the globe, inspired by last year's ruckus in Seattle and a continuing series of confrontations. One international organization after another has scurried to catch up with the popular rebellions against globalization by announcing "initiatives" to promote human rights, the environment and worker protections. Leading multinationals have been eager to sign up as co-sponsors, since the new codes or compacts are all voluntary and toothless. If corporate declarations of good intent were edible, the world's hungry would be fed.

The purpose obviously is public relations—improving the tarnished images of global corporations and portraying weak-willed international institutions as attentive and relevant to the turmoil of worldwide controversy. But even empty gestures can prove to be meaningful, sometimes far beyond what their authors had in mind. An enduring truth, a wise friend once explained to me, is that important social change nearly always begins in hypocrisy. First, the powerful are persuaded to say the appropriate words, that is, to sign a commitment to higher values and decent behavior. Then social activists must spend the next ten years pounding on them, trying to make them live up to their promises or persuading governments to enact laws that will compel them to do so. In the long struggle for global rules and accountability, this new phase may be understood as essential foreplay.

William Greider, "Waking Up the Global Elite," *The Nation*, October 2, 2000

6

Assessing A16

Michael Albert

Congratulations are in order for the organizers of the April 16-17 protests in Washington. First, issues of IMF/World Bank-imposed poverty, powerlessness, and ecological and social devastation were elevated to moral and economic visibility. Subway car drivers told riders about the anti-IMF demonstrations while bypassing certain stations. Comprehensive teach-ins were held in many venues. Images of thousands upon thousands of A16 activists were seen worldwide. CNN even had Robert Weissman brilliantly explaining the events in a repeatedly shown headline news report. This and more is great progress.

Second, the IMF and World Bank dissent also addressed Third World poverty, the situation of farmers and laborers abroad and in the United States, political prisoners, the debt, consumerism, ecology, issues of race and gender, and much more. Constituencies with narrower political agendas worked with those who had broader ones, and vice versa. There was mutual understanding and support. The AFL-CIO leadership, individual unions, mainstream green organizations, U.S. Jubilee 2000, A16, and Black Bloc groups had political differences, but these differences were well-managed by organizers on all sides. This too is great progress.

Third, the various tactical wings of the movement—whether seeking to get arrested, to militantly protest, to make a public but peaceful statement, or just to learn or teach—worked together marvelously. Diverse tactics did not trump one another. Tension was minimal. Intercommunication was considerable. Coalitions were strengthened rather than dissolving into tactical disputes. There was in-the-street mutual aid, careful planning of venues and events, and pre-demonstration communication of aims. The Black Blocs brought to the actions tactical energy, creativity, and courage, as in Seattle, but now also considerable willingness to blend these attributes into the larger venue respecting the desires of other constituencies and actively defending their less-prepared fellow participants. It was a praiseworthy transformation in a very short period. Likewise, activists personally dedicated to nonviolence openly respected those advocating different tactical views. Tactical differences remain, as do political differences, but all are being constructively handled, which is great progress.

Fourth, the numbers of people ready to actively engage in or support lawbreaking was stupendous—there were more people trained and ready for civil disobedience in D.C. than in Seattle. At the height of the 1960s protest movement, the Washington Mayday demonstration attempted to use civil disobedience to shut down Washington, D.C. The numbers were hard to assess, but roughly 20,000 people attended. In contrast, April 16th was only the second major U.S. gathering about global economics. It wasn't a product of a long and steadily escalating struggle deep into its development, yet roughly 20,000 people went to D.C. to risk or provoke arrest, or support such choices. The civil disobedient part of the Global Economics movement is way ahead of schedule.

Fifth, many who attended A16 perhaps felt the logistics of the days of confrontation were a defeat for the demonstrators. This wrongly snatches defeat from the jaws of victory. No one should be surprised that the U.S. government can amass an effective coercive force to control events in the streets of Washington, D.C. Yes, the Washington police had a very effective strategy. They used illegitimate, preemptive arrests, set out a huge restricted area around the World Bank and IMF keeping activists from even the vicinity of their focus of dissent, invaded and closed the Convergence Center as intimidation, used a mixture of arrests, aggression, and sometimes even forbearance in an effective brew to try to channel outcomes, and worked hard to goad protesters into acting out, though unsuccessfully.

Activists countered with a fledgling but steadily growing nonviolent army: mobile, determined, decentralized, antiauthoritarian, learning while doing, yet nonetheless holding its own. No doubt we can learn many new lessons for the future, but the key realization we must highlight is that to judge demonstrations by narrow tactical norms is wrong on two counts. First, this is not a realm where we should expect outright victories anytime soon. And second, it just isn't the point. The point is to raise consciousness, to increase dissent, to solidify awareness and skills, to create ties and solidarity, to raise the image to elites (and ourselves) of a trajectory of dissent that will steadily enlarge, solidify, and diversify unless demands are granted. The victory on the streets of Washington was in the discipline, organization, steadfastness, creativity, and insight of the demonstrators doing their best against a powerfully armed, mobile, highly-trained force whose sole purpose was to keep them at bay and demoralize them. The victory was in accomplishing the priority goals of consciousness raising and solidarity and bringing the issues to the public. The fact that the pin-striped bankers' meetings were not totally terminated is a side-bar matter.

Sixth, the overall media coverage in Washington, D.C. was better than in Seattle. The media doesn't have new values, much less new structures, of course. Instead, strong watchdog and alternative media work have created a context in which the public knows too much and is able to get information from too many sources for the media to distort certain realities too sharply without getting condemned for it. This could be seen at almost every level including major TV coverage, CNN, *The Washington Post*, *The New York Times*, and lesser, more local newspapers and media. Of course the coverage wasn't perfect, very far from it, but what else is new? The point is, coverage improved over Seattle due to the pressures brought to bear by media activism and alternative sources and the growing power and visibility this movement has. This was another victory, and one that should fuel further pressure against mainstream media and for alternative media creation.

Each time we protest we ought to gain new insights. So here are some things we might want to think about. Why were the numbers of union members and of representatives from religious communities who might have participated in the public legal events such as the Jubilee 2000 rally (April 9), and the AFL-CIO/Citizens' Trade Campaign rally (April 12) lower, rather than much higher, than they were in Seattle? Was this due to diminished organizing of these constituencies? Was it due to a fear of what the situation might be like? If so, what could have been done to alleviate such fears and to provide congenial venues for folks not prepared to run in the streets, or get arrested? Having 8,000 people for A16 civil disobedience and another 12,000 for A16 militant support gains full power when there are another 100,000 for legal peaceful assembly and marching, and to keep repression at bay. It won't do to repeatedly assemble the militant and experienced leg of the movement, if a more massive peaceful leg isn't present as well. To stand tallest, we need both.

Why were communities of color largely absent from the legal peaceful demonstrations and overwhelmingly absent from the civil disobedience demonstrations and the leadership throughout? Acknowledging A16's sincere efforts to incorporate these communities as participants and leaders, plus the presence of Free Mumia constituencies, what more needs to be done to have more success? Does it just take time, so we need to continue efforts already in place and the work will begin to show serious results? Is it in part due to a very warranted difference in expectations of handling at the hands of police, and if so, what is to be done about that? Do global economics organizers need to organizationally and personally offer movements that oppose antiracist police violence the kind of support that we want their organizations and members to provide global economics efforts? It shouldn't surprise anyone if that turns out to be a precondition for serious trust and solidarity.

Young constituencies were overwhelmingly the backbone of the A16 demonstrations and provided a powerful display of growing youth radicalization, yet the issue of outreach arises for young people too. Why could young people amass 10,000 to 20,000 activists from campus and youth constituencies to take substantial risks—an amazing achievement—yet not amass another 100,000 from those same constituencies for legal, peaceful, participation for people just getting politicized, or trying to learn, or angry but not yet inclined to do civil disobedience? Why were almost all the young folks veteran radicals, with so few rookies present?

For campus militants and radicals to meet together, rally themselves, organize themselves, and educate themselves, is excellent. To gather and hang out for mutual support and even entertainment is excellent too. But what matters as well, is for radicals to go into their neighbor's dorms or apartments, into the libraries, the dining halls, and even the fraternities, gymnasiums, bars, and malls, to organize people who don't yet agree. Labor and religious organizations, large environmental groups, women's organizations, youth groups, and antiracist groups need to reach into their constituencies and educate and organize to get new people who don't yet see the importance of participating. The movement should not be typified by attaining a certain scale and then operating more or less in cultural, social, and political separation from the rest of one's community, campus, neighborhood, city, or workplace. Reaching into new arenas where folks disagree with our efforts is the core task of effective organizing.

So while we all should rightly and vigorously celebrate the wonderful achievements of A16, we also ought to be thinking about future protests and about whether outreach to labor, religious communities, people of color, and young people who don't yet agree about the issues is getting sufficient energy and creativity.

We already know that this movement is top-notch regarding its capacity for planning and carrying out events that committed radicals can engage in with great impact and organizational success. Now let's massively enlarge our base.

Poor Majority Criticizes Rich Minority

The "Group of 77" (representing 133 developing nations) held a three-day summit in Havana, Cuba in mid-April 2000 and issued statements supportive of protesters outside the World Bank/IMF meetings in Washington.

Many third world leaders accused the rich nations of imposing economic structures and policies that drain resources from the poor majority to the wealthy minority. "Never has the world witnessed such massive disparities in international social and economic activities," said Nigerian President Olusegun Obasanjo, who chaired the summit. He warned that failure to reform international aid policies that have maintained the wealth gap "constitute a major threat to international peace and security."

Malaysian Prime Minister Mahathir denounced "rogue currency traders" who plunged his country and other East Asian countries into financial crisis by undermining their currencies. "Millions were thrown out of work and made destitute," he said. " The international economic institutions moved in ostensibly to help with loans but in reality to facilitate the takeover of the country's economy and even politics." He proposed that rich countries allow free flows of labor as well as capital. "If money is capital for the rich, labor is the capital of the poor countries," he said. "They should be allowed to migrate to the rich countries to compete for the jobs there just as the powerful corporations of the rich must be allowed to compete with their tiny counterparts in the poor countries."

7

The Power of the People

Alli Starr

A t one of the final spokescouncil planning meetings for the action in Washington, D.C., activist/author Starhawk asked a crucial question: "What is victory?" Throughout the church packed with over 500 activists from around the world, voice after voice inspired us with the ways in which we had already won. The room filled with applause as we acknowledged the formation of new alliances and national networks across the United States; the development of solidarity with revolutionaries from all over Africa, Asia, and Latin America; and thousands of activists now trained in nonviolent direct action, street theater, jail solidarity, consensus decision making, media messaging, medical safety, and the spokescouncil affinity group model of decentralized organizing. Most importantly, the gathering proved that thousands of U.S. activists were joining the international movement against the International Monetary Fund, the World Bank, and the World Trade Organization, bringing hope to our allies in the "Global South." Our creativity and commitment helped to lift the veil of secrecy around these criminal institutions and their devastating effect on the lives of working people worldwide.

We are moved to compare our success in D.C. with the anti-WTO action in Seattle. Though we did not *stop* the World Bank/ IMF meetings in D.C., we should consider what was accomplished. Before April 2000, few North Americans knew of the

IMF, the World Bank, and their role in the global economy. Their biannual meetings have, for the most part, gone unnoticed. For weeks before and after the A16 action, however, the issues made front-page news. Institutions and policies that Americans are not supposed to understand or care about are finally being discussed. Many Americans are now questioning the validity of these powerful institutions. Throughout the world, the WTO, IMF, and World Bank are seen as the latest manifestation of the colonizers and imperialists. While more Americans are now rising up to say, "50 years is enough!", indigenous communities, and people of color all over the world are saying, "500 years is enough!"

The power of people willing to put their bodies on the line to protest these institutions has changed the terms of the debate. The fact that delegates to the IMF/World Bank meetings seriously discussed issues such as debt forgiveness and the African AIDS epidemic is a testament to our work in building a mass mobilization. These undemocratic institutions have been dragged out into the light. On the streets of D.C., bus drivers, homeless folks, students, and other local residents wanted to know more about the IMF and the World Bank, and many thanked us for being in their city.

The Mobilization for Global Justice built bridges with various local communities leading up to the action. We were invited into dozens of schools and community centers to talk with diverse audiences—from kindergartners to senior citizens—about the IMF and World Bank. People shared their frustration with evictions in poor neighborhoods, corporate takeovers, longer working hours, prison expansion, the lack of democracy, and the growing gap between the rich and the poor, domestically and globally. Many had recently heard of the WTO, but not the IMF. It was easy to connect sweatshops and environmental degradation in other countries with the loss of jobs and toxic waste disposal in America's inner cities. After a puppet workshop we offered to five- and six-year-olds, one charter school principal told me that Channel 7 news had tried to get him to complain about us. He told them, on the contrary, that his teachers intended to use some of our facilitation techniques, and that our visit had been one of the most fun and informative days of the year for the students and staff.

The Security Response of an Insecure Elite

For four days central Washington, D.C. was locked down. Universities and major institutions were closed. On April 16, over 20,000 activists took to the streets, shutting down the center of the nation's capital. As in Seattle, we held tight blockades, we sang, chanted, and danced, and we carried hundreds of giant puppets and banners. We protected each other, formed affinity group clusters, learned each other's nicknames, and made consensus decisions in large groups. Many veterans of mass direct actions shared their expertise; as a result, A16 was remarkably well organized.

On A16 and A17, in order to ensure that the IMF and World Bank meetings would take place, police were forced to sneak delegates in during the middle of the night. Even then, some delegates—most notably the French finance minister—could not get through our blockade and missed meetings. Police officers I spoke with were doing forty-hour shifts to maintain the huge perimeter around the IMF and World Bank buildings. This "no-protest zone" was intended to shut out our voices and deny us our First Amendment rights.

Some activists were pepper sprayed in the face at close range and some were badly beaten. In all, some 1,300 nonviolent activists were arrested; hundreds maintained jail solidarity (mass noncooperation with authorities) even when beaten, coerced, threatened with rape, lied to, and denied bathrooms, food, and water. Due to the strength of the activists and the use of solidarity tactics, most were finally released with $5 fines.

The corporate media, predictably, attempted to dilute the movement's achievements in Washington. Those of us who were involved should be clear about our many successes. Although those in power want us to feel diminished, we must take into account at what expense the bankers were able to meet. We ended the secrecy and we educated millions. We shut down the heart of the capital and we empowered a new generation of activists.

Every one of us in D.C. represented at least twenty more who supported our efforts but couldn't be there themselves. Support demonstrations were held in hundreds of towns and cities worldwide. Our movement for global justice is growing exponentially.

The perpetrators of greed and violence can no longer hide in obscurity while they carry out their deceptive policies. While we must be critical of and learn from past actions, let us not be deceived about the powerful and courageous work done during the A16 protests. We must measure our success by looking at the movement as a whole, and remember our struggle for justice is larger than one action, and often longer than a generation. Let us acknowledge nonetheless how much we have accomplished, even in the past few years, in building a movement against corporate globalization.

We are honored to be part of a long line of nonviolent, direct action social justice movements. We stand in solidarity with the tea tossers in Boston, with the women who fought for 150 years to vote, with those who would not be moved from lunch counters and bus seats in the civil rights movement, with the labor activists who went on strike for eight-hour days and workers' rights, with students who burned draft cards and resisted the Vietnam War, with the blockaders who prevented nuclear power plants from being built, with the gentle warriors who put their bodies on the line to protect our last remaining ecosystems, and all of the courageous people throughout history who have taken power into their own hands to fight for every freedom we are now struggling to preserve and expand.

THE BREATHTAKING GENIUS OF THE FREE MARKET

GIANT DUTCH CONGLOMERATE UNILEVER BUYS **BOTH** BEN & JERRY'S ICE CREAM AND **SLIMFAST**...

NOW I GET COUPONS SO THAT THE MORE "CHUNKY MONKEY" I EAT THE MORE I SAVE ON SLIMFAST!

...DEMONSTRATING ONCE AGAIN HOW CORPORATE CONSOLIDATION IS GOOD FOR CONSUMERS. WHAT MORE CAN BE AHEAD?....

BEANO INC, THE ANTI-FLATULENT, BECOMES A WHOLLY OWNED SUBSIDIARY OF **BIG SKY CHILI CORPORATION**

R.J.R. RESEARCH LABS

IF WE CRANK UP THE NICOTINE IN OUR SMOKES AND DIAL DOWN THAT IN THE PATCH ....WE CAN KEEP PEOPLE ON BOTH!

YOU'RE A GENIUS!

GAS

MOBILEXXON SEES THE PROFIT IN GLOBAL WARMING AND BUYS UP INTERCONTINENTAL AIR CONDITIONING INC.

BUY GAS AND WIN YOUR OWN AIR CONDITIONER

REYNOLDS TOBACCO BUYS UP **ACME HEALTH CORP** MAKER OF "NICOFIEND" THE POPULAR NICOTINE PATCH TREATMENT.

M. WUERKER

Section Two:

Why the World Bank and the IMF Suck

This section details the many crimes of these two institutions and shows why a growing number of individuals and organizations around the world have joined the movement to transform or eliminate these financial behemoths.

In "We Either Unite or We Die" Fidel Castro gives a critical overview of the global economy and proposes some far-reaching courses of action.

Robert Weissman answers "Twenty Questions About the IMF" and provides convincing arguments as to why this institution should be downsized.

A group of prominent scholars, parliamentarians, and activists got together to issue "A Letter to the U.S. Congress" calling on legislators to use the considerable clout of the U.S. government to change IMF/World Bank policies regarding debt, the environment, and the lack of openness of these institutions.

Soren Ambrose ("Congress Takes Action Against User Fees") exposes how the World Bank/IMF policy of requiring impoverished countries to charge "user fees" for access to healthcare and education caused members of Congress to threaten cutting off funds if the practice continues.

In "Zimbabwe's Crisis Justifies World Bank/IMF Protests,"

Patrick Bond traces the roots of that country's economic woes to policies written in Washington.

"Warning: World Bank Destroys Forests" by Korinna Horta utilizes internal documents to expose the fact that, despite promises of reform, the World Bank still facilitates deforestation.

In "End the World Bank's Corporate Welfare Programs!" the 50 Years Is Enough Network exposes two of the World Bank Group's less well-known branches (the International Finance Corporation and the Multilateral Investment Guarantee Agency) and how they work against majority interests.

Charlie Cray ("The World Bank's Revolving Door") exposes the close sharing of personnel between the World Bank and transnational corporations.

In "Silencing Joseph Stiglitz" veteran journalist David Moberg explains why a former top economist at the World Bank agrees with many of the criticisms made by anti-World Bank protestors.

Nicola Bullard weighs in with "Collateral Damage at the World Bank," which reveals the manuevering behind the scenes by U.S. Treasury Department officials that resulted in the resignation in protest of Professor Ravi Kanbur, the main author of the World Bank's *Development Report 2000*.

Concluding the section is Madeleine Bunting's "Bank Chief and Bishops Clash," which shows that the head of the World Bank is opposed by even some of the most mainstream moral authorities on the planet.

8

We Either Unite or We Die

Fidel Castro

The largest grouping of third world countries in the United Nations is the Group of 77 (G77), formed in 1964 and now numbering 133 countries. In mid-April 2000, these nations, representing the majority of the world's people, met in Havana, Cuba, and issued a proclamation harshly critical of the policies of the World Bank and the International Monetary Fund. The following speech by Cuban President Fidel Castro was met with thunderous applause at the G77 Summit, but the U.S. press failed to cover Castro's speech or the other criticism coming from the G77.

Never before has humankind had such formidable scientific and technological potential, such extraordinary capacity to produce riches and well-being, but never before have disparity and inequity been so profound in the world.

Technological wonders that have been shrinking the planet in terms of distances and communications coexist today with the increasingly wider gap separating wealth and poverty, development and underdevelopment.

Globalization is an objective reality underlining the fact that we are all passengers on the same vessel: This planet where we all live. But passengers on this vessel are traveling in very different conditions.

Trifling minorities are traveling in luxurious cabins furnished with cell phones and access to the Internet and global communication networks. They enjoy a nutritious, abundant, and balanced diet as well as clean water supplies. They have access to sophisticated medical care and to culture.

Overwhelming and hurting majorities are traveling in conditions that resemble the terrible slave trade from Africa to America in our colonial past. Eighty-five percent of the passengers on this ship are crowded into its dirty hold, suffering hunger, disease, and helplessness.

The Heads of State meeting here, who represent the overwhelming and hurting majorities, have not only the right but the obligation to take our rightful place at the helm to ensure that all passengers can travel in conditions of solidarity, equity, and justice.

Free Market Dogma

For two decades, the Third World has been repeatedly listening to only one simplistic discourse, and one single policy has prevailed. We have been told that deregulated markets, maximum privatization, and the state's withdrawal from economic activity are the infallible principles conducive to economic and social development. The developed countries, particularly the United States, the big transnationals benefiting from such policies, and the International Monetary Fund have designed in the last two decades a world economic order that is hostile to poor countries' progress and that is not sustainable in terms of the preservation of society and the environment.

Two decades of so-called neoliberal structural adjustment have left behind economic failure and social disaster. Under neoliberal policies the world economy experienced global growth between 1975 and 1998 which hardly amounted to half that attained between 1945 and 1975 with Keynesian market regulation policies and active participation in the economy by governments.

In Latin America, where neoliberalism has been applied with strict adherence to doctrine, economic growth in the neoliberal stage has been lower than that attained under the previous state development policies. After World War II, Latin America had no debt but today we owe almost $1 trillion. This is the highest per capita debt in the world. The income disparity between the rich and the poor in the region is the greatest worldwide. There are more poor, unemployed, and hungry people in Latin America now than at any other time in its history.

Under neoliberalism the world economy has not been growing faster in real terms; however, there is more instability, speculation, external debt, and unequal exchange. Likewise, there is a greater tendency to financial crises occurring more often, while poverty, inequality, and the gap between the wealthy North and the dispossessed South continues to widen.

Crises, instability, turmoil, and uncertainty have been the most common words used in recent years to describe the world economic order.

The deregulation that comes with neoliberalism and the liberalization of capital movements have a deep negative impact on a world economy where speculation blooms in currency markets and derivative markets, and mostly speculative transactions amount to no less than $3 trillion *daily*.

Our countries are urged to be more transparent with their information and more effective with bank supervision but financial institutions like the hedge funds fail to release information on their activities, are unregulated, and conduct operations that exceed all the reserves kept in the banks of the South countries.

In an atmosphere of unrestrained speculation, the movements of short-term capital make the South countries vulnerable to any external contingency. The Third World is forced to immobilize financial resources and grow indebted to keep hard currency reserves in the hope that they can be used to resist the attack of speculators. Over twenty percent of the capital revenues obtained in the last few years were immobilized as reserves but they were not enough to resist such attacks as proven by the 1997 financial crisis in Southeast Asia.

Presently, $727 billion from the world Central Banks' reserves are in the United States. This leads to the paradox that with their reserves the poor countries are offering cheap long-term financing to the wealthiest and most powerful country in the world while such reserves could be better invested in economic and social development.

Demand Removal of the IMF

Cuba has successfully carried out education, healthcare, culture, science, sports, and other programs—despite four decades of economic blockade—and revalued its currency seven times in the last five years in relation to the U.S. dollar. This has been thanks to Cuba's privileged position as a *nonmember* of the International Monetary Fund.

A financial system that keeps forcibly immobilized enormous resources, badly needed by the countries to protect themselves from the instability caused by that very system that makes the poor finance the wealthy, should be removed.

The International Monetary Fund is the emblematic organization of the existing monetary system and the United States enjoys veto power over its decisions. As far as the latest financial crisis is concerned, the IMF showed a lack of foresight and a clumsy handling of the situation. It imposed its conditioning clauses that paralyzed the governments' social development policies thus creating serious domestic hazards and preventing access to the necessary resources when they were most needed.

It is high time for the Third World to strongly demand the removal of an institution that neither provides stability to the world economy nor works to deliver preventive funds to the debtors to avoid their liquidity crises; rather, it protects and rescues the creditors.

Where is the rationale and the ethic of an international monetary order that allows a few technocrats, whose positions depend on American support, to design in Washington identical economic programs for implementation in a variety of countries to cope with specific Third World problems?

Who takes responsibility when the adjustment programs bring about social chaos, thus paralyzing and destabilizing nations with large human and natural resources, as was the case in Indonesia and Ecuador?

It is of crucial importance for the Third World to work for the removal of that sinister institution, and the philosophy it sustains, to replace it with an international financial regulating body that would operate on democratic bases and where no one has veto power; an institution that would not defend only the wealthy creditors and impose interfering conditions, but would allow the regulation of financial markets to stop unrestrained speculation.

A viable way to do this would be by establishing—not a 0.1 percent tax on speculative financial transactions as Mr. Tobin brilliantly proposed—but rather a minimum one percent tax that would permit the creation of a large fund, in excess of $1 trillion every year to promote sustainable and comprehensive development in the Third World.

The Debt Has Already Been Paid

The underdeveloped nations' external debt already exceeds $2.5 trillion and during the 1990s it increased more dangerously than in the 1970s. A large part of that new debt can easily change hands in the secondary markets; it is more dispersed now and more difficult to reschedule.

As we have been saying since 1985: The debt has already been paid, if note is taken of the way it was contracted, the swift and arbitrary increase of the interest rates on the U.S. dollar in the 1980s and the decrease of basic commodity prices—a fundamental source of revenue for developing countries. The debt continues to feed on itself in a vicious circle whereby money is borrowed to pay interest on old debt.

Today, it is clearer than ever that the debt is not an economic but a political issue, therefore, it demands a political solution. It is impossible to continue overlooking the fact that the solution to this problem must come from those with resources and power, that is, the wealthy countries.

The so-called Heavily Indebted Poor Countries Debt Reduction Initiative (HIPC) exhibits a big name but small results. It can only be described as a ridiculous attempt at alleviating 8.3 percent of the South countries' total debt. Almost four years after its implementation only four countries among the poorest thirty-three have navigated the complicated process simply to condone the negligible figure of $2.7 billion, which is one-third of what the United States spends on cosmetics every year.

Today, the external debt is one of the greatest obstacles to development and a bomb ready to blow up the foundations of the world economy at any time during an economic crisis.

The resources needed for a solution that goes to the root of this problem are not large when compared to the wealth and the expenses of the creditor countries. Every year $800 billion is used to finance weapons and troops, even after the Cold War is over, while no less than $400 billion go into narcotics, and additional billions go into commercial publicity that is as alienating as narcotics.

As we have said before, realistically speaking, the Third World countries' external debt is unpayable and uncollectible.

World Trade

In the hands of the rich countries, world trade is an instrument of domination. Under neoliberal globalization trade has perpetuated inequalities and provided a venue for settling disputes among developed countries for control over present and future markets.

The neoliberal discourse recommends commercial liberalization as the best and only formula for efficiency and development. While neoliberalism keeps repeating its discourse on the opportunities created by trade openings, the poor countries' participation in world exports was lower in 1998 than in 1953. Brazil, with an area of 3.2 million square miles, a population of 168 million and $51.1 billion in exports during 1998, is exporting less than The Netherlands with an area of 12,978 square miles, a population of 15.7 million and exports of $198.7 billion that same year.

Trade liberalization has essentially consisted of the unilateral removal of protection instruments by the South. Meanwhile, the developed nations have failed to do the same to allow Third World exports to enter their markets.

The wealthy nations have fostered liberalization in strategic sectors associated with advanced technology—services, information technology, biotechnology, and telecommunications—where they enjoy enormous advantages that deregulated markets tend to augment.

On the other hand, agriculture and textiles, two particularly significant sectors for our countries, have not even been able to remove the restrictions agreed upon during the Uruguay Round because this is not of interest to developed countries.

In the OECD [Organization for Economic Cooperation and Development], the club of the wealthiest, the average tariff applied to manufactured exports from underdeveloped countries is four times higher than that applied to the club member countries. A real wall of tariff and nontariff barriers is thus raised that excludes products of the South countries.

Basic commodities are still the weakest link in world trade. In the case of sixty-seven South countries such commodities account for no less than fifty percent of their export revenues. The neoliberal wave has wiped out the defense schemes contained in the terms of reference for basic commodities. The supreme dictum of the marketplace cannot tolerate any distortion, therefore the Basic Commodities Agreements and other formulas designed to address unequal exchange were abandoned. It is for this reason that today the purchasing power of such commodities as sugar, cocoa, coffee and others is twenty percent of what it used to be in 1960; consequently, sales revenue does not even cover production costs.

A special and differentiated treatment for poor countries has been considered, not as an elementary act of justice and a necessity that cannot be ignored, but as a temporary act of charity. Actually, such differential treatment would not only recognize the enormous differences in development that prevent the use of the same yardstick for the rich and the poor but also a colonial past that demands compensation.

Significance of the Revolt in Seattle

The failed WTO meeting in Seattle showed that neoliberal policies are generating intensified opposition among more and more people, in both South and North countries. The United States of America presented the Round of Trade Negotiations that should have begun in Seattle as a higher step in trade liberalization, regardless of its own aggressive and discriminatory Foreign Trade Act still in force. That Act includes provisions like the "Super-301", a real display of discrimination and threats to apply sanctions to other countries for reasons that go from the assumed opposition of barriers to American products to the arbitrary and often cynical judgements made by the U.S. government regarding the human rights situation in other countries.

In Seattle there was a revolt against neoliberalism. Its most recent precedent had been the refusal to accept the imposition of a Multilateral Agreement on Investments (MAI). This shows that the aggressive market fundamentalism, which has caused great damage to our countries, has found a strong and deserved world rejection.

The Technology Gap

In a global economy where knowledge is the key to development, the technological gap between the North and the South tends to widen with the increasing privatization of scientific research and its results.

The developed countries with fifteen percent of the world's population presently concentrate eighty-eight percent of Internet users. There are more computers in the United States than in the rest of the world put together. Rich countries control ninety-seven percent of patents globally and receive over ninety percent of international licensing rights, while for many South countries the exercise of the right to intellectual property is nonexistent.

In private research, the lucrative element takes precedence over necessity; the intellectual property rights leave knowledge out of reach for underdeveloped countries, and the legislation on patents does not recognize know-how transfer or the traditional property systems, which are so important in the South. Private research focuses on the needs of wealthy consumers.

Vaccines have become the most efficient technology to keep healthcare expenses low since they can prevent diseases with one dosage. Because they yield low profits, however, vaccines are put aside in favor of medications that require repeated dosages and yield higher financial benefits.

The new medications, the best seeds, and, in general, the best technologies have become commodities whose prices can be afforded only by the rich countries.

The murky social results of this neoliberal race to catastrophe are in sight. In over one hundred countries the per capita income is lower than fifteen years ago. At the moment, 1.6 billion people are faring worse than at the beginning of the 1980s.

Over 820 million people are undernourished and 790 of them live in the Third World. It is estimated that 507 million people living in the South today will not live to see their 40th birthday.

In the Third World countries represented here, two out of every five children suffer from growth retardation and one out of every three is underweight; 30,000 who could be saved are dying every day; 2 million girls are forced into prostitution; 130 million children do not have access to elementary education and 250 million minors under fifteen are forced to work. The world economic order works for twenty percent of the population but it leaves out, demeans and degrades the remaining eighty percent.

We cannot simply accept to enter the next century as the backward, poor, and exploited rearguard; the victims of racism and xenophobia prevented from access to knowledge, and suffering the alienation of our cultures due to the foreign consumer-oriented message globalized by the media.

As for the Group of 77, this is not the time for begging from the developed countries or for submission, defeatism, or internecine divisions. This is the time to recover our fighting spirit, our unity and cohesion in defending our demands.

Fifty years ago we were promised that one day there would no longer be a gap between developed and underdeveloped countries. We were promised bread and justice; but today we have less and less bread and more injustice.

The world can be globalized under the rule of neoliberalism but it is impossible to rule over billions of people who are hungry for bread and justice. The pictures of mothers and children under the scourge of droughts and other catastrophes in whole regions of Africa remind us of the concentration camps in Nazi Germany; they bring back memories of stacks of corpses and moribund men, women, and children.

Another Nuremberg is required to put on trial the economic order imposed on us: a system that is killing of hunger and curable diseases more men, women, and children every three years than all those killed by World War II in six years.

In Cuba we usually say: "Free Homeland or Death!" At this Summit of the Third World countries we would have to say: "We either unite and establish close cooperation, or we die!"

The full text of Castro's speech and other documents of the G77 South Summit can be found on the website www.G77.org.

Our loyalties must transcend our race, our tribe, our class, and our nation; and this means we must develop a world perspective.

Rev. Martin Luther King, Jr.

9

Twenty Questions on the IMF

Robert Weissman

1. What is the IMF's mission and how has it changed over time?

The International Monetary Fund (IMF) was created in 1944 to maintain the standard of fixed exchange rates that was established at the end of World War II. Since the abandonment of the gold standard in 1971, the IMF has adopted a new core mission, providing loans to economically troubled countries.

Countries with balance of payment difficulties—meaning their earnings from imports and other sources are insufficient to pay off their foreign debts—turn to the IMF for two reasons. First, the IMF provides loans to cover immediate obligations to foreign creditors. Second, private lenders and other public lenders, such as the World Bank, generally will not lend to troubled economies unless they have a loan agreement with the IMF.

Thus the IMF plays a "gatekeeper" role: If you are a poor, indebted country, you can't get access to foreign credit unless you have a deal with the IMF. Agreements with the IMF typically require countries to adopt "structural adjustment" policies as the condition for a loan.

2. What is structural adjustment?

Structural adjustment is a policy package in line with what is often called "neoliberalism," a far-reaching version of the "free trade" agenda. In many ways, it is a harsh version of Newt Gingrich's *Contract with America*.

The central goals of structural adjustment are to open up countries to having transnational corporations get access to their workers and natural resources, shrink the size and role of government, rely on market forces to distribute resources and services, and integrate poor countries into the global economy.

Key structural adjustment policies include: privatizing government-owned enterprises and government-provided services, slashing government spending, orienting economies to promote exports, liberalizing trade and investment rules, raising interest rates, increasing taxes, and eliminating subsidies on consumer items such as food, fuel, and medicines.

3. What is the relationship between the IMF and World Bank? How has that changed over time? Do their functions overlap?

The World Bank was also formed in 1944 to help with European postwar reconstruction. It later shifted its focus to assisting development efforts in the Third World. It has funded major infrastructure projects: roads, hydroelectric dams, coal plants, and other major investments that private capital would not initiate because they are not profitable. These projects have been highly controversial for their effect on the environment, indigenous people, rural communities, and women.

Starting in the 1980s, and while continuing to do project lending, the Bank began shifting its loans toward structural adjustment and sectoral adjustment loans. About two-thirds of the Bank's lending now goes for structural adjustment and sectoral adjustment. The World Bank's structural adjustment programs are not appreciably different than those of the IMF.

The IMF and World Bank jointly administer a program, now called the Heavily Indebted Poor Country/Poverty Reduction and Growth Fund, that provides very modest debt relief to the world's poorest countries on the condition that they undergo years of structural adjustment.

The World Bank respects the IMF's unofficial gatekeeper role, and generally will not make loans to countries that have not received an IMF seal of approval.

4. What is the IMF's and the World Bank's relationship to the World Trade Organization (WTO)?

The IMF, World Bank and the WTO all share a commitment to "free trade" and binding developing countries into the global economy. The WTO, which implements agreements governing world trade and administers a binding mechanism to resolve trade disputes between nations, generally operates independently of the IMF and World Bank.

In November 1999, however, the IMF, the World Bank and the WTO announced a new "coherence agreement" in which they pledged to coordinate future activity. It is unclear what this will mean in practice, but some fear the IMF and World Bank may incorporate some of the worst elements of WTO agreements into their lending conditions.

5. How does the IMF set its policies?

The IMF is governed primarily by an executive board that consists of representatives of IMF member countries, with voting weighted in favor of those countries that provide more money to the Fund. The executive board sets broad policy and approves loans. The agency's bureaucracy handles the massive, day-to-day operations and exerts a strong, *de facto* influence over policy.

Voting at the IMF is weighted, with bigger contributing countries having proportionally more say. The United States—the largest shareholder at the IMF with more than 17 percent of the votes—maintains effective veto power over major decisions at the Fund. In practice, the U.S. Treasury Department exercises overwhelming control at the IMF; *The New York Times* has referred to the IMF as a "proxy for the United States."

6. How open is the IMF to outside scrutiny and participation?

Although "transparency" (openness) is a favorite buzzword in development circles, the IMF is extremely secretive in its operations. In recent years, as criticism of the IMF's secrecy has grown in developing countries, the IMF has made public "Policy Framework Papers"—the documents establishing the parameters of structural adjustment programs in specific countries—and some other important materials. These are all papers that a few years ago the IMF said it could not make public out of respect for the sovereignty of the countries they affected. Meanwhile, other critical documents remain secret.

Although the IMF assumes a dominating role in economies undergoing structural adjustment—with IMF officials often posted in national finance departments—precise IMF demands are concealed from the affected populations. As a general matter, the IMF does not seek public input into the policies it imposes on borrowing countries.

7. Given that the U.S. taxpayer contributes large amounts of money to the IMF, what kind of oversight of the IMF is provided by Congress or other agencies?

The IMF is generally viewed as following a policy line set by the U.S. Treasury Department. Congressional efforts to influence policy at the Fund have generally failed. Congress has directed the U.S. Executive Director to the IMF to use "voice and vote" to push for certain reforms, but this has had virtually no effect on IMF policy. Almost all decisions at the IMF are reached by consensus, and recorded votes are rarely taken. The U.S. Executive Director to the IMF, Karen Lissakers, told a Congressional committee in 1998 that the Fund's executive board had taken votes on approximately a dozen out of 2,000 decisions taken during her tenure. The only time Congress has affected IMF policy is when it refused to provide requested funding increases.

8. How do IMF policies benefit transnational corporations?

Structural adjustment policies open up developing countries to foreign investors on terms most favorable to transnational corporations. Structural adjustment requires countries to remove barriers to foreign investment, and push countries to orient their economies to producing exports—typically produced by or sold to transnational companies. State-owned enterprises privatized under structural adjustment are frequently sold to transnationals, often at bargain-basement prices.

IMF-orchestrated bailouts—assistance to countries whose exchange rates are plummeting—provide money primarily so that developing countries can pay off their foreign creditors (including private banks). Many critics view these bailouts as bailouts of the creditors who don't absorb the cost of risky loans gone bad.

This particular kind of corporate welfare can have especially pernicious effects, since it may encourage excessively risky lending by bankers and others. If they know they have free, *de facto* insurance from the IMF, they can make very risky loans at high interest rates without fear of paying for failures.

9. What is the IMF's approach to helping countries that are deeply in debt?

The IMF program for helping poor countries that are deep in debt was, until recently, called the Enhanced Structural Adjustment Facility (ESAF). In 1999, under fire for a program poorly run, the Fund changed the name to Poverty Reduction and Growth Facility (PRGF). This program is operated in conjunction with the World Bank's Heavily Indebted Poor Country (HIPC) Initiative.

The purpose of PRGF/HIPC is to provide some debt relief— that is, to cancel *part* of the debts—for poor countries that have no hope of paying back their total foreign debt and for whom debt payments are draining their economy.

However, the debt relief under PRGF/HIPC is very modest. Under the plan, many countries find that while the absolute amount of their debt may decline, the amounts they actually pay are only minimally affected. That is because many poor countries cannot make their debt payments, and, often with the agreement of their creditors, they pay just a portion of what they owe.

Compounding the problem, the price of receiving debt relief under the PRGF/HIPC program is to implement a supervised structural adjustment program for three years (previously six years) prior to receiving any debt relief.

10. What would the alternative be?

An alternative would call for immediate debt cancellation of the debts of the poorest countries and far-reaching debt cancellation for other developing countries. For less poor countries, debt cancellation could focus on "odious" debt—debt incurred by dictators, military regimes or for boondoggle projects pushed by foreign interests. This cancellation would come without any structural adjustment conditions.

Many economic justice advocates from developing countries urge conditions related to the establishment of democracy, or a commitment to devote resources to meeting the basic needs of the poorest segments of society. (See Chapter 26.)

In the case of the poorest nations, debts could be cancelled by drawing on the existing resources of the IMF and World Bank, that is, without rich countries providing these institutions with any new funding.

Beyond approaches to debt cancellation, many in the developing world are also calling for an alternative approach to economic development. One of the demands arising from grassroots movements is respect for a diversity of national approaches, so there would be no "blueprint" for development to parallel the IMF's cookie-cutter structural adjustment policies. But there is growing agreement about the importance of a number of principles: national food security, land reform, devoting attention to production for local needs, an emphasis on egalitarian wealth distribution, emphasizing smaller enterprises, empowering workers and respecting worker rights, imposing regulations on foreign capital to limit a country's exposure to volatile international capital markets, involving civil society in development planning, and preserving a substantial role for government in planning, regulating, and carrying out economic activity.

11. What are the economic and social impacts of structural adjustment?

Structural adjustment has been successful at its goal of reducing the scope of government and integrating developing countries into the global economy. Yet it has failed by many other measures. Most countries undergoing structural adjustment have not experienced economic growth, even in the medium term.

Those developing countries that have experienced the greatest economic successes in recent decades have violated many of the central precepts of structural adjustment. They have protected certain parts of their economy, and they have maintained an active government role in economic planning.

An external review of ESAF programs sponsored by the IMF illustrated the basic failure of structural adjustment. Countries undergoing ESAF-sponsored structural adjustment experienced stagnating growth rates and saw their foreign debt nearly double: dramatic evidence of failure, since reducing foreign debt is one of ESAF's ostensible purposes.

In the two regions with the most structural adjustment experience (Latin America and Africa), per capita income has stagnated in Latin America, and collapsed in Africa, where per capita income dropped more than 20 percent between 1980 and 1997.

The emphasis on exports tends to be socially disruptive, especially in rural areas. Poor subsistence farmers frequently find their economic activity described as nonproductive, and they experience land pressures from expanding agribusiness, timber companies, and mines. Pushed off their land, they frequently join the ranks of the urban unemployed, or move onto previously unsettled, and often environmentally fragile, lands.

Structural adjustment has generally contributed to rising income and wealth inequality in the developing world, a fact tacitly acknowledged by both recently retired IMF Managing Director Michel Camdessus and World Bank President James Wolfensohn.

12. How did the Asian financial crisis of 1997 start and what was the IMF's response?

The Asian meltdown was caused in large part by a heavy reliance on short-term foreign loans by South Korea, Thailand, the Philippines, Malaysia, and Indonesia. When it became apparent that private enterprises in those nations would not be able to meet their payment obligations, international currency markets panicked. Currency traders converted their Asian money into dollars, and the Asian currencies plummeted. That made it harder for the Asian countries to pay their loans, and it made imports suddenly very expensive.

There were other underlying causes for the financial crisis, including overinvestment in real estate and other speculative and unnecessary ventures, but almost everyone agrees that the currency crash and financial disaster were vastly disproportionate to the weaknesses in the Asian economies.

The IMF treated the Asian financial crisis like other situations where countries could not meet their balance of payment obligations. The Fund made loan arrangements to enable countries to meet foreign debt payments (largely to private banks in these cases) on the condition that the recipient countries adopt structural adjustment policies.

But the Asian crisis differed from the normal situation of countries with difficulties paying off foreign loans. For example, the Asian governments were generally not running budget deficits. Yet the Fund instructed them to cut spending: a recessionary policy that deepened the economic slowdown.

The Fund failed to manage an orderly roll-over of short-term loans to long-term loans, which was most needed, and it forced governments, including those in South Korea and Indonesia, to guarantee private debts owed to foreign creditors.

In retrospect, even the IMF admits that it made things worse in Asia. Malaysia stood out as a country that refused IMF assistance and advice. Instead of further opening its economy, Malaysia imposed capital controls, and sought to eliminate speculative trading in its currency. While the IMF mocked this approach when adopted, the Fund later admitted that it had succeeded. Malaysia generally suffered less severe economic problems than the other countries embroiled in the Asian financial crisis, and rebounded faster from its recession.

13. Did the 1997-1998 global financial crisis lead to a shift in the debate surrounding structural adjustment policies in the developing world?

The IMF's structural adjustment prescriptions for countries suffering through the Asian financial crisis were roundly denounced, including by many conservative and mainstream economists and opinion makers. The widespread criticism of the Fund undermined its political credibility.

The IMF response has been to make some minor concessions in making its documents more publicly available, increasing its rhetorical commitment to poverty in its structural adjustment programs, and by limiting its demands that countries liberalize their capital markets (e.g., by allowing unlimited trading in their currency, and permitting foreign investors to invest in domestic stocks and bonds without restriction).

14. What were the consequences of the Asian financial crisis in countries like Thailand and Indonesia? Did IMF policies help those countries?

The financial crisis led to massive human suffering. In South Korea, a country whose income was approaching European levels, unemployment skyrocketed from approximately 3 percent to 10 percent. "IMF suicides" became common among workers who lost their jobs and dignity.

In Indonesia, the worst hit country, poverty rates rose from an official level of 11 percent before the crisis to 40 to 60 percent in varying estimates. Gross Domestic Product (GDP) declined by 15 percent in one year. In September 1998, UNICEF reported that more than half the children under two years old in Java, Indonesia's most populous island, were suffering from malnutrition. At one point, the food shortage became so severe that then-President B.J. Habibie implored citizens to fast twice a week. Many had no choice.

IMF-mandated reductions in government spending worsened the Asian recession. The forced elimination of price controls and government subsidies for the poor imposed enormous costs on the lowest income strata. In Indonesia, food and gasoline prices rose 25 to 75 percent overnight or in the course of a few days.

An October 2000 study by 25-year veteran IMF economist Morris Goldstein found that "both the scope and the depth of the Fund's conditions were excessive." Goldstein concluded that his fellow policymakers at the IMF "clearly strayed outside their area of expertise."

15. What has been the IMF's role in Russia?

Russia in the 1990s has witnessed a peacetime economic depression of unprecedented scale. Much of the blame for this social and economic catastrophe rests with the IMF, which has had a central role in designing and supervising Russia's economic policy since 1992.

The number of Russians in poverty has risen from 2 million to 60 million since the IMF came to post-Communist Russia. Male life expectancy has dropped sharply from 65 years to 57. Economic output is down by at least 40 percent.

The IMF's "shock therapy"—sudden and intense structural adjustment—helped bring about this disaster.

"In retrospect, it's hard to see what could have been done wrong that wasn't," Mark Weisbrot of the Center for Economic and Policy Research told a Congressional committee in late 1998. "First there was an immediate decontrol of prices. Given the monopoly structure of the economy, as well as the large amount of cash savings accumulated by Russian households, inflation soared 520 percent in the first three months. Millions of people saw their savings and pensions reduced to crumbs."

Then the IMF and Russian policymakers compounded their mistakes, Weisbrot explained. "In order to push inflation down, the authorities slammed on the monetary and fiscal brakes, bringing about a depression. Privatization was carried out in a way that enriched a small class of people, while the average person's income fell by about half within four years."

Meanwhile, Russia kept its economy functioning with an influx of foreign funds, loaned at astronomically high interest rates because of the strong possibility of default. In 1998, with the Asian crisis still unfolding and with Russian default seemingly near, the IMF agreed to a $23 billion loan package to Russia, seeking to maintain the ruble's overvalued exchange rate. An initial $4.8 billion portion of the loan left Russia immediately— some used to pay off foreign lenders, much of it stolen by Russian politicians. Soon after, the ruble collapsed anyway.

For the IMF, the prospect of Russia deciding to continue not to repay loans was extremely worrisome. To avert this problem, the Fund continued its loan program, but its loans to Russia didn't actually go to Russia; IMF money disbursed to Russia was and is held at the IMF to pay off prior IMF loans to Russia.

Does the IMF think it made fundamental mistakes in Russia? No. From the IMF's perspective, the problem has been *not enough* IMF-style reform. Here's how former IMF Managing Director Michel Camdessus put it in September 1999: "[Russia's economic] shortcomings represent not so much the failure of reform as the effects of 70 years of central planning and the incomplete implementation of reform policies—itself a result of a lack of domestic political consensus on reform."

16. How do IMF programs affect workers?

As outgoing World Bank economist Joseph Stiglitz says, the IMF views labor as just another commodity. One IMF priority has been promoting "labor flexibility," meaning making it easier for workers to be fired. The Fund has supported regulatory changes to remove restrictions on government and private employers firing or laying off workers.

The IMF has actively promoted government downsizing, even though in many countries the government is the major employer and there are few prospects for alternative employment.

The IMF also views many worker benefits as too costly (if they are provided by the government) or too inefficient (if required of private employers). It has urged major scaling back of government pension programs around the world.

The IMF has also called for reducing minimum wages in

countries such as Haiti. Respect for the workers' right to organize is not included in the structural adjustment policy package.

17. To what extent do IMF/World Bank structural adjustment policies incorporate environmental considerations? How do structural adjustment policies impact the environment?

"The IMF claims to defer to the World Bank on environmental matters, but promotes export-led development that has major environmental impacts without asking the World Bank for any formal assessment of the environmental implications of its approach," explains Friends of the Earth in a recent report, *IMF: Selling the Environment Short.*

"The World Bank has failed to provide environmental guidance to the IMF, and is even delinquent in assessing the environmental impacts of its own structural adjustment loans," Friends of the Earth concludes. "A recent internal World Bank study found that fewer than 20 percent of World Bank adjustment loans included any environmental assessment."

But the failure to consider environmental implications does not mean there aren't any. Here is how Friends of the Earth summarizes the effects of structural adjustment on the environment: "The IMF's economic policies affect the environment in various ways. One major goal of structural adjustment programs (SAPs) and stabilization programs is to generate foreign exchange through a positive trade balance. To meet the IMF's ambitious targets for currency reserves and trade balance, countries must quickly generate foreign exchange, often turning to their natural resource base. Countries often overexploit their resources through unsustainable forestry, mining and agricultural practices that generate pollution and environmental destruction, and ultimately threaten future exchange earnings."

"Exports of natural resources have increased at astonishing rates in many countries under IMF adjustment programs, with no consideration of the environmental sustainability of this approach. Furthermore, the IMF's policies often promote price-sensitive raw resource exports, rather than finished products. Finished products would capture more added value, employ more people in different enterprises, help diversify the economy, and disseminate more know-how."

"Structural adjustment and stabilization also aim to generate positive government budget balances. In the effort to rapidly trim budget deficits, governments are forced to make choices, and inevitably, the environment loses. Lower spending weakens a government's ability to enforce environmental laws, and diminishes efforts to promote conservation. In addition, governments are told to increase private investment and to reduce the role of the state in favor of private sector development. Budget priorities are often directed toward business promotion, creating a further strain on cash-strapped environmental enforcement agencies. Governments may also relax environmental regulations to meet structural adjustment program objectives of increasing foreign investment, as occurred in the case of the Philippines."

As an example of how IMF-mandated budget cuts hurt the environment, Friends of the Earth points to the Brazilian Amazon: "Because of IMF budget restrictions, as of July 1999, funding for the enforcement of environmental regulations and supervision programs was reduced by over 50 percent."

18. What is the Meltzer Commission and what did it say?

The Meltzer Commission, formally known as the International Financial Advisory Commission to the U.S. Congress, was created by the 1998 U.S. legislation that allocated an additional $18 billion to the IMF. The Commission was charged with reviewing the operations of the IMF and World Bank, and making recommendations for changes in the international financial institutions. The Commission, which included both Republican and Democratic appointees, unanimously agreed on two points: the debts of the forty-one most indebted and impoverished countries should be cancelled; and the IMF should get out of the business of long-term development lending.

Commission members split over how severely the IMF's functions should be limited (with most Democratic members aiming to preserve a broader role for the IMF), and over proposed changes for the World Bank. Eight of the eleven Commission members supported a proposal to change the World Bank to the World Development Agency, to eliminate the Bank's lending function, replace Bank loans with grants, and generally to shrink the size of the Bank.

19. Given the international nature of markets, does structural adjustment indirectly affect the U.S. economy even if the United States is not directly forced to structure our economy in response to IMF guidelines?

Structural adjustment in poor countries and trickle-down economics in richer countries such as the United States reinforce one another. Just as structural adjustment carries the U.S. system of privatized, fee-for-service health care to the Third World, those seeking to privatize the U.S. social security system point to Chile's social security system as a model.

More concretely, structural adjustment forces developing countries to orient their economies to produce exports. The primary target for those exports is the United States, and secondarily, other rich countries. The IMF and World Bank economic programs do not support regional trade.

The IMF model of unregulated global economic integration places countries in competition with each other to produce goods with the lowest possible wage bill. That puts downward pressure on wages in all countries, including countries such as the United States (particularly in markets like steel and textiles that are produced in both rich and poor countries).

20. What should Congress do to reform/abolish the IMF/World Bank? What could the IMF do to promote sustainable development?

Were the IMF actually concerned about sustainable development, there are various policy measures it could promote. Friends of the Earth has called on the IMF to emphasize ecological taxes rather than value-added taxes, among other measures.

Some organizations, including some members of the Jubilee 2000 coalition in the United States, have called on the IMF to pay more attention to poverty and the effect of its lending on the poor. They place hope in the IMF's newly stated commitment to address poverty in its lending practices, and hope that the re-naming of the Economic Structural Adjustment Facility—now the Poverty Reduction and Growth Facility—will signal more than just a name change.

Others, however, believe the IMF is irredeemable. They be-lieve the emphasis should not be on pushing the IMF to adopt better policies, but on finding ways to shrink the IMF's influ-ence and power, so it has less say over developing country poli-cies. This group is loathe to support more funding for the IMF, even funding that is supposed to be allocated for debt relief. In-stead, they say, the IMF should draw on its existing resources to enact immediate debt cancellation for the poorest countries. And, if the Fund is to continue at all, they call on IMF lending to be delinked from structural adjustment conditions.

There is growing support for the idea of limiting the IMF's reach. Even U.S. Treasury Secretary Lawrence Summers has urged that the Fund be restructured so that it cease engaging in long-term development lending—the sort of lending done to the poorest countries, invariably with structural adjustment condi-tions attached. The Meltzer Commission echoed this position, as has the head of the German central bank.

The very logic and framework of structural adjustment poli-cies require the repression of democratic rights. This is because these policies demand drastic fiscal, monetary, and economic measures which cannot help but raise very strong reactions from the public. And such reactions have to be repressed. This is a joint production of the international finance community with the cooperation of local elites and leaders in our own country. The majority of the people are shut out of the negotiations.

Leonor Briones, President,
Freedom from Debt Coalition, Philippines

10

A Letter to the U.S. Congress

*Noam Chomsky, Walden Bello,
Dennis Brutus, et al.*

*The following letter, drafted in early 2000 by a group
of individuals and organizations critical of World Bank/
IMF policies, was sent to all members of Congress calling
for no increase in the quota of money allocated to the IMF.*

The undersigned organizations and individuals from around
the world are opposed to any increase in the size, power,
or funding of the International Monetary Fund, and in particular are opposed to any increase in the quota of member countries. The disastrous impact of IMF-imposed policies on workers' rights, environmental protection, and economic growth and
development; the crushing debt repayment burden of poor countries as a result of IMF policies; and the continuing secrecy of
IMF operations provide ample justification for denying increased
funding to the IMF.

Economic Growth and Development

The IMF's overwhelming preference for high interest rates
and fiscal austerity, even in the absence of any economic justification, has caused unnecessary recessions, reduced growth, hin-
dered economic development, and increased poverty throughout
the world. There is now a consensus among economists that the
IMF's recent intervention in the Asian financial crisis actually
worsened its impact. Many believe that the Fund bears the pri-

mary responsibility for turning the financial crisis into a major regional depression, with tens of millions of people being thrown into poverty with no end in sight.

Labor

IMF policies undermine the livelihood of working families. IMF policies have mandated mass layoffs by companies and changes in labor law to facilitate or encourage mass layoffs, as happened recently in South Korea. IMF policies regularly force countries to lower wages, or undermine efforts by governments to raise wages—as, for example, in Haiti in recent years.

Environment

IMF policies encourage and frequently require the lowering of environmental standards and the reckless exploitation of natural resources in debtor countries. The export of natural resources to earn hard currency to pay foreign debts under IMF mandates damages the environment while providing no benefit to poor and working people in debtor countries.

Debt

IMF and World Bank policies have forced poor countries to make foreign debt service a higher priority than basic human needs. The World Bank claims that it is "sustainable" for countries like Mozambique to pay a quarter of their export earnings on debt service. Yet after World War II, Germany was not required to pay more than 3.5 percent of its export earnings on debt service. Poor countries today need a ceiling on debt service similar to the one Germany had. According to U.N. statistics, if Mozambique were allowed to spend half of the money on healthcare and education that it is now spending on debt service, it would save the lives of 100,000 children per year.

Openness of IMF Operations

IMF policies that affect the lives of a billion people are negotiated in secret, with key conditions not released to the public.

The people who bear the burden of these policies often do not even have access to the agreements that have been negotiated.

The policies of the IMF have undermined the ability of developing countries to provide for the needs of their own peoples. Such an institution should not be expanded.

Thank you for your consideration of our concerns.
Sincerely,
Walden Bello, Focus on the Global South, Bangkok
Carlos Heredia, Congressman, Mexico
Dennis Brutus, Jubilee 2000 Africa
Noam Chomsky, Massachusetts Institute of Technology
Friends of the Earth
50 Years is Enough Network
Essential Action
Development Group for Alternative Policies
Preamble Center for Public Policy

What's under attack is a culture that rewards loan-making for its own sake, solicits little input from the local citizenry, favors huge infrastructure projects over direct poverty alleviation, and ignores the often devastating effects of its projects (the Sardar Sarovar Dam in India, to name but one horror story, threatens to displace a million or so people). But numbers speak loudest: By the [World] Bank's own reckoning, nearly sixty percent of its projects are failures. In Africa, its track record is virtually unblemished by success.

Jerry Useem
Fortune magazine, May 15, 2000

11

Congress Takes Action Against IMF/World Bank User Fees

Soren Ambrose

In a landmark move, the U.S. House of Representatives in early July 2000 approved a measure to pressure the International Monetary Fund and the World Bank to stop requiring that impoverished countries charge "user fees" for access to primary health services and primary education.

The anti-user fees measure was included in the Foreign Operations appropriations bill approved by the full House. It was originally introduced as an amendment in committee by Rep. Jesse Jackson, Jr. (D-IL), a staunch advocate for debt cancellation and economic justice for impoverished people around the world. The House action represents the first time that Congress has required the IMF and World Bank to change the specific conditions they impose on borrowing countries.

User fees—charges imposed for using a health clinic or attending school—have led to increased illness, suffering, and death when people cannot pay for health services, and decreased school enrollments when poor families can no longer afford to send their children to school. In a tragic example in Zambia quoted by UNICEF, a researcher observed a fourteen-year-old boy with acute malaria turned away from a health clinic for want of a thirty-three cent registration fee. According to the report, "within two hours, the boy was brought back dead."

The requirement that the world's poorest countries charge fees for primary health and education has long been one of the most controversial features of the austerity programs mandated by the IMF and World Bank. Advocates for the abolition of the fees point to scores of studies which demonstrate that their imposition forces a society's most impoverished families to deny their children basic education and their sick and dying healthcare.

Although James Wolfensohn, President of the World Bank, has contended in addressing members of Congress that the Bank has abandoned user fee requirements, current documents, such as the program for Tanzania linked to the granting of limited debt relief, contradict his stance.

Under the provision adopted by the House, beginning in 2002, U.S. funding would be provided only when the heads of the World Bank and IMF certify their institutions "will not include user fees or service charges through 'community financing,' 'cost sharing,' 'cost recovery,' or any other mechanism for primary education or primary healthcare, including prevention and treatment efforts for AIDS, malaria, tuberculosis, and infant, child, and maternal well-being" in any of their programs.

Actress Valerie Harper, a RESULTS Board member and one of the leading advocates of abolishing user fees, argued to members of Congress that charging the world's most impoverished people for basic health and education was a "terrible tragedy." She pointed out, "I live in one of wealthiest areas of the wealthiest country in the world, and my daughter can attend Beverly Hills High School for free. Meanwhile, women in the poorest countries of sub-Saharan Africa are told they have to come up with hard cash to send their kids to first grade or see a doctor at a clinic. We must not accept this."

Njoki Njoroge Njehu, a Kenyan who directs the 50 Years Is Enough Network, a coalition of U.S. groups opposing IMF and World Bank policies, said, "This significant step by the House brings closer the day when people throughout the Global South will be able to decide on their own priorities. We do not want to raise another generation on promises from the IMF and World Bank that the sacrifice of their education and health will be 'short-term pain for long-term gain.'"

Recent studies have revealed some of the damage done by user fees imposed by IMF/World Bank structural adjustment programs:

• In Kenya, introduction of a 33-cent fee for each visit to outpatient health centers led to a 52 percent reduction in outpatient visits. After the fee was suspended, visits rose 41 percent.

• Introduction of user fees at rural clinics in Papua New Guinea led to a decline of about 30 percent in attendance, and although it subsequently increased, it never returned to pre-fee levels. Health workers also reported a reduction in completion rates for courses of treatment.

• In Dar es Salaam, Tanzania, three public hospitals saw attendance drop by 53.4 percent between the second and third quarters of 1994, when user fees were introduced.

• In Nicaragua, about one-fourth of primary school children have not enrolled in primary school since charges for registration and a monthly stipend were introduced.

• In Niger, cost recovery measures implemented as part of a structural adjustment program between 1986 and 1988 had the following results: 1) a sharp decline in already very low primary school enrollment rates which went from 28 percent in 1983 to 20 percent in 1988; 2) a drop in utilization of preventative care services; 3) increased exclusion of the most impoverished from care at Niamey Hospital, where outpatients who did not pay for care waited an average of 24 days before seeking care while an outpatient who did have to pay for care waited an average of 51 days; and 4) exemption systems that were applied to the benefit of military, and civil service families and not for the intended beneficiaries (the most impoverished).

• UNICEF reports that in Malawi, the elimination of modest school fees and uniform requirements in 1994 caused primary enrollment to increase by about 50 percent virtually overnight—from

1.9 million to 2.9 million. The main beneficiaries were girls. Malawi has been able to maintain near full enrollment since then.

Editor's Note: On October 25, 2000, the U.S. Senate passed the Foreign Operations Appropriations bill containing the anti-user fee provisions discussed in this chapter. When this is signed into law by the President it will force a significant change in IMF/World Bank policy—as a result of grassroots pressure!

Paying a Big Price for Education

The World Bank is the largest source of money for education programs in the poorest countries. In the 1990s the Bank boosted loans for education, but increased funding is not always matched by better results. The World Bank found that the failure rate for its education loans had increased from 11.8 percent of the portfolio in 1992 to 17.5 percent in 1994. Also, many countries are suffering under huge debt burdens as well as structural adjustment policies which force them to slash education subsidies.

Tanzania, half of whose population is illiterate, was recently forced to introduce school fees under a structural adjustment program. The policy led to a drop in primary and secondary school enrollment. Tanzania now spends a third of its budget on debt payments, roughly four times what it spends on primary education. Tanzania is not alone. In sub-Saharan Africa the percentage of 6-11 year-olds enrolled in school fell from nearly 60 percent in 1980 to less than 50 percent in 1990.

The World Bank and IMF have also forced countries to crack down on teachers. In Kenya, the IMF told the government that it would not approve a promised loan if the government gave in to demands from striking teachers to raise salaries from the average basic salary of $150 per month. The teacher strikes were supported by 70 percent of the population. Kenya is heavily indebted, and pays 25 percent of its revenue on debt service, compared to 6.8 percent on education.

Data from www.whirledbank.org.

12

Zimbabwe's Crisis Justifies World Bank/IMF Protests

Patrick Bond

In Zimbabwe, President Robert Mugabe appears to have taken leave of his senses, potentially plunging his country of twelve million into civil war. What does this have to do with the mid-April 2000 protests against the World Bank and International Monetary Fund?

Confusingly, Mugabe excels in IMF-bashing, famously telling Fund staff to "Shut up!" in late 1999. Yet from independence in 1980 until quite recently, he followed their advice unfailingly. Indeed, just five years ago, Zimbabwe was Washington's newest African "success story," as Harare adopted economic policies promoted by World Bank and IMF lenders, and even conducted joint military exercises with the Pentagon.

Things fell apart quickly. Southern African diplomats are shaking their heads in frustration at Mugabe's quick-shattering promises—made to Thabo Mbeki and other local leaders—to tone down racial rhetoric, reverse land invasions of 1,000 white farms, and sort out financial matters with Britain, IMF, and donor governments. Is Mugabe deranged, or instead playing out a tragic logic partially of his own making, but partially imposed from above?

Under the very real threat of losing parliament to the labor-led Movement for Democratic Change in mid-2000 elections, he resorted to authoritarian populism: egging on a few thousand land invaders so as to restore memories of the 1965-80 struggle against Rhodesian colonialism, a period when his Zimbabwe African National Union (ZANU) truly represented a mass, popular movement dedicated to reversing settler-colonial land ownership.

Yet early on, perceptive ZANU watchers identified two major problems: the party's class character and its likely realignment towards foreign capital. Political scientist Rudi Murapa (currently president of Africa University, Zimbabwe's second-largest) wrote in 1977 of an alliance between "a politically ambitious petit-bourgeois leadership, a dependent and desperate proletariat and a brutally exploited and basically uninitiated peasantry." Forecast Murapa, "After national liberation, the petit-bourgeois leadership can abandon its alliance with the workers and peasants and emerge as the new ruling class by gaining certain concessions from both foreign and local capital and, in fact, forming a new alliance with these forces which they will need to stay in power. Of course, lip service commitment, à la Kenya, to the masses, will be made."

Accusations that ZANU "sold out" are justifiable, technically—given not only the steady rise in corruption, but the fact that most of the land and other wealth redistributed since 1980 has gone to ZANU cronies not the masses—yet merely crying "sell out" is deeply unsatisfying. The same will be said of the African National Congress, as it was in Zambia of Kenneth Kaunda and likewise his successor Frederick Chiluba. However, assailing petit-bourgeois acquisitiveness—which also motivated white Zimbabweans to loot their compatriots' land and labor beginning in 1890—risks downplaying the second factor: the role of global financial pressure.

Once anti-Rhodesia financial sanctions were lifted, Zimbabwe made bad policy choices and succumbed to arm twisting by Washington. Finance minister Bernard Chidzero (who later chaired the IMF/Bank Development Committee) borrowed massively at the outset, figuring that repayments—which required

16 percent of export earnings in 1983—would, he insisted, "decline sharply until we estimate it will be about four percent within the next few years. The main lender, the World Bank, concurred: "The debt service ratios should begin to decline after 1984 even with large amounts of additional external borrowing." This was the economic equivalent of a sucker-punch, for in reality, Zimbabwe's debt servicing spiraled up to an untenable 37 percent of export earnings by 1987.

Loan conditions quickly emerged. By 1985, the IMF pressured Mugabe to cut education spending, and in 1986 food subsidies fell to two-thirds of 1981 levels. Similarly, genuine land reform was stymied not only by the "willing-seller, willing-buyer" compromise with Ian Smith's Rhodesians at Lancaster House, but by the World Bank's alternative: showering peasants with unaffordable micro-loans. From a tiny base in 1980, the Bank's main partner agency granted 94 000 loans by 1987. But without structural change in agricultural markets, the Bank strategy floundered, as 80 percent of borrowers defaulted in 1988 notwithstanding good rains.

Analyst Ibbo Mandaza lamented in 1986, "International finance capital has, since the Lancaster House Agreement, been the major factor in the internal and external policies of the state in Zimbabwe." Agreed Thandike Mkandawire, head of the Geneva-based United Nations Research Institute for Social Development, "It seems the government was too anxious to establish its credentials with the financial world."

The macroeconomic situation worsened when Chidzero persuaded Mugabe to ditch Rhodesian-era regulatory controls on prices and foreign trade/financial flows, liberalizing the economy through an Economic Structural Adjustment Programme (ESAP) in 1991. ESAP was supposedly "homegrown," but World Bank staff drafted much of the document, which was substantively identical to those imposed across Africa during the 1980s-90s. ESAP brought immediate, unprecedented increases in interest rates and inflation, which were exacerbated (but not caused) by droughts in 1992 and 1995. As money drained from the country, the stock market plummeted by 65 percent in late 1991 and manufacturing output declined by 40 percent over the subsequent four years. Amazingly, the Bank's 1995 evaluation of ESAP declared it "highly satisfactory" (the highest mark possible).

More vulnerable than ever before, Zimbabwe's currency then came under fierce attack during the 1997 East Asian crisis, falling 74 percent during one four-hour raid after Mugabe joined the conflict in the Democratic Republic of the Congo (formerly Zaire) and paid generous pensions to protesting liberation war veterans. Reacting to growing unpopularity and two Harare food riots, Mugabe finally invoked three pro-poor policies in 1997-98: reimposition of price controls on staple foods, conversion of corporate foreign exchange accounts to local currency, and steep luxury import taxes. (He also foolishly cemented the Zimbabwe dollar's value too high.)

The IMF and donors are explicitly withholding hard currency until these three policies are reversed. So Zimbabwe spends its hard currency repaying foreign lenders, and can't afford to import petroleum. The harder the economic pressure bites, the more Mugabe staggers politically.

What lessons from Harare? Evade hard-selling foreign bankers. More aggressively—and honestly—redistribute wealth and land. And avoid structural adjustment policies that worsen inequality, stagnation and vulnerability.

Will leaders in the Movement for Democratic Change, and for that matter also in Pretoria, take heed? Regardless, more protesters—including Harare's church-based, anti-debt activists—are joining the global campaign to shut down the IMF and the World Bank, precisely because of mounting evidence of this kind, from Zimbabwe and across the Third World.

The most powerful weapon in the hands of the oppressor is the mind of the oppressed.

Steven Biko

13

Warning: World Bank Policies Destroy Forests

Korinna Horta

Destruction of the world's tropical, temperate, and boreal forests has continued unabated over the past decade, with consequences no longer in dispute. Hundreds of millions of people who rely wholly or in part on the use of forests for their livelihoods are put at risk. Agriculture is suffering as local climates are changing with the advance of savannas and deserts. The world's terrestrial biodiversity, predominantly found in tropical forests, is increasingly at risk. In addition, deforestation worldwide is estimated to contribute about 20 percent of the greenhouse gases now released into the atmosphere.

Virtually all tropical forests are located in developing countries, and no single global institution plays a bigger role in developing countries than the World Bank. It is well documented that the World Bank has fostered forest destruction through support for commercial logging, road-building through forested areas and megadams that flood large expanses of forest.

Environmentalist campaigns in the 1980s against the World Bank's contribution to forest destruction led to a rethink at the Bank. In 1991, the Bank published a Forest Policy paper ending Bank support for commercial logging in primary forests and promising a new approach that would emphasize conservation, poverty reduction and support for the rights of local people.

In November 1999, the World Bank's internal review agency,

the Operations Evaluation Department (OED), published a review of the Bank's implementation of its 1991 Forest Policy Paper. The OED report documents that the Bank's performance has been a flop. "Bank influence on containing rates of deforestation in tropical moist forests has been negligible in the 20 countries identified for Bank focus," the report concludes.

The OED finds that the World Bank has largely ignored the guidelines provided in the Forest Policy Paper, and that it has paid little attention to the impacts of its loans on forests. Most strikingly, the OED report identifies the economic policies promoted by World Bank structural adjustment programs as being among the driving forces of deforestation—meaning the Bank is making the problem worse.

In a break from previous World Bank studies, the OED report does not blame poor farmers and "slash and burn" agriculture for deforestation, nor is demographic pressure mentioned as a major underlying cause of forest loss. The new report declares globalization, economic policies designed to promote exports, bad governance, corruption, and out-of control logging companies to be the driving forces of deforestation in the world.

Structural Adjustment and Deforestation

Some of the policies identified by the OED report as being harmful to forests, such as trade liberalization and export promotion, lie at the very heart of the World Bank's structural adjustment lending.

Structural adjustment loans are made to governments in exchange for their commitment to adopt a set of policy changes, including promotion of exports and opening up to foreign investment. In 1999, for the first time in the World Bank's history, the volume of structural adjustment loans was larger than the volume of regular project loans, representing more than 50 percent of the institution's approximately $30 billion annual lending in fiscal year 1999.

The OED highlighted a range of structural adjustment measures that contribute to deforestation. "Policies associated with economic crisis and adjustment—such as devaluation, export incentives, and removal of price controls—tend to boost production of tradable goods, including agricultural and forestry products. In doing so, and without mitigatory measures, they encourage forest conversion," the report states. "Further, constrained fiscal situations may lead to reduced public spending on environmental protection and weaken the capacities of forest ministries to enforce laws and regulations."

Yet the OED report concludes that "the Bank has made little progress in addressing the impacts of adjustment lending on the forest sector." In a few cases, the Bank has added to structural adjustment packages special conditionalities to protect forests. The OED report found, however, that these measures "lack credibility," because building capacity and institutions require long-term efforts and agreement from national governments.

While emphasizing the distinction between the processes of globalization and Bank adjustment lending, Uma Lele, an adviser in the World Bank's OED and the chief author of the November report, says that "the Bank's own adjustment lending must do a better job of environmental impact assessment." Noting the technical difficulty in conducting such an analysis (as compared to environmental assessments for project loans), she says that she is relatively optimistic that the Bank will move in this direction. World Bank officials did not respond to requests by this author for comment on the OED report.

Broken Promises

The 1991 Forest Policy Paper emphasized the importance of respect for indigenous peoples' rights and local community participation in project development. With some caveats, environmental and development organizations applauded this policy as a break from the past and as offering hope for a more holistic Bank approach to the world's forests. The Forest Policy instructed World Bank staff that all types of investments, including infrastructure construction and energy and mining projects, had to take into account their potential impacts on forests. It also required that the World Bank's investment plans for a country, known as country assistance strategies, and all economic sector work consider possible impacts on forests.

Yet the 1991 policy's promise has not been met, the OED report finds. After reviewing hundreds of project documents, the OED study concludes that the Forest Policy has largely been ignored at all levels and that forest-related World Bank lending has done little to alleviate poverty.

While "plans for incorporating participation in Bank projects have become more ambitious," the report states, "implementation has lagged." The report cites five "weaknesses" to account for this implementation failure: "inadequate reflection of social, technical, institutional and political realities on the ground in project design; omission of key stakeholders during project preparation and implementation; inadequate time and resources allowed to develop genuine participatory approaches; lack of sufficient expertise in participatory techniques among Bank staff and consultants; and poor choice of monitoring and evaluation indicators." In addition, it found that the Bank had neglected governance issues and that its activities in the area of institution building had been weak.

Despite claims of being a "Knowledge Bank," the World Bank is frequently oblivious to the local political, economic, and social realities in regions affected by its projects. The OED report states that "crucial information" on land tenure (land ownership arrangements) is frequently missing from key Bank documents, even though this information is essential to respect and protect indigenous rights and to advance effective conservation schemes.

Which Way for the Bank?

The OED report reveals that a whole decade has been lost in which the world's forests could have benefited from improved protection. In order to address the problem, the OED report urges the creation of incentives to ensure that Bank staff have the necessary resources and can be held accountable for implementing forest policy guidelines.

Environmentalists were stunned by other OED recommendations, which they found entirely divorced from the report's findings. Many environmentalists believe senior World Bank staff whose goal is to increase lending for forestry projects significantly influenced these recommendations.

The OED report claims that the prohibition of direct financing for logging in moist primary tropical forests has had the effect of discouraging innovative investments in forestry, implying that investments in logging can save forests. Furthermore, it claims that the prohibition has led to a "chill" in overall lending for forestry, even though, as the OED itself documents, annual Bank lending for forestry-related projects has increased by 78 percent since adoption of the Forest Policy Paper in 1991. In fact, a specific policy directive published in 1993 created an enormous loophole allowing direct support for logging under special circumstances which are not defined in detail.

The OED's Uma Lele says that the OED review shows that in individual cases the Bank is funding important forest projects that facilitate both conservation and poverty elimination, especially in tree-poor countries. In China, she says, Bank-supported tree planting may absorb one fifth of the country's carbon emissions. "It would be a mistake to throw out the baby with the bath water," she says, in arguing for increased funding.

Environmental and development NGOs have emphasized that small-scale community-based logging on a pilot basis might provide valuable learning experiences about how to manage forests sustainably for the benefit of local people. But, citing the extensive recent record of failure, they have resolutely opposed large-scale industrial forestry in the tropics. Industrial systems, they insist, cannot sustain timber yields over time, much less protect ecosystems and biodiversity. And as the OED report acknowledges, industrial forestry has done nothing to improve the livelihoods of local communities.

In the years ahead, will the World Bank follow the implicit recommendations in the OED report's findings? Will it strengthen the 1991 Forest Policy Paper to provide added focus on boreal forests in Russia which, since the end of the Cold War, have increasingly been a target for World Bank investments? Or will the Bank instead open the floodgates for new large-scale industrial forestry investments, accelerating global deforestation?

The Lawrence Summers Memo

The memo from which the following was excerpted was written by Treasury Secretary Lawrence Summers, who was then chief economist at the World Bank.

December 12, 1991

'Dirty' Industries: Just between you and me, shouldn't the World Bank be encouraging MORE migration of the dirty industries to the LDCs [Less Developed Countries]?

1) The measurements of the costs of health impairing pollution depends on the foregone earnings from increased morbidity and mortality. From this point of view a given amount of health impairing pollution should be done in the country with the lowest cost, which will be the country with the lowest wages. I think the economic logic behind dumping a load of toxic waste in the lowest wage country is impeccable and we should face up to that.

2) The costs of pollution are likely to be non-linear as the initial increments of pollution probably have very low cost. I've always thought that under-populated countries in Africa are vastly UNDER-polluted, their air quality is probably vastly inefficiently low [sic] compared to Los Angeles or Mexico City. Only the lamentable facts that so much pollution is generated by non-tradable industries (transport, electrical generation) and that the unit transport costs of solid waste are so high prevent world welfare enhancing trade in air pollution and waste.

14

End the World Bank's Corporate Welfare Programs!

50 Years Is Enough Network

During the 1990s, the World Bank Group (WBG) saw that private corporations were investing more in some middle-income "developing" countries at the same time as governments were cutting aid budgets. Rather than focus on making up the shortfall to the most impoverished countries, the Bank is determined to jump in front of the investment parade. It is not enough, it seems, that the rules it imposes through its (and the IMF's) notorious structural adjustment programs force markets open for corporations and ensure them a supply of cheap labor and commodities. So the WBG is devoting more attention and resources to its division that lends directly to private corporations, the International Finance Corporation (IFC), and has assigned it the task of devising the WBG's overall "Private Sector Development Strategy."

The Private Sector Development Strategy aims to further the interests of the private sector, including its expansion "into areas traditionally the preserve of governments" in Southern countries, such as "health and education services." But the IFC's record in fighting poverty and protecting the environment is abysmal, and it is even less accountable to the public than the other components of the World Bank Group. Rather than having its influence expand, the IFC should be abolished, along with the Bank's other private sector arm, the Multilateral Investment Guarantee Agency

(MIGA) which provides investment insurance for transnational corporations. An impressive consensus on this recommendation is now emerging, one that ranges from conservative economists advising the U.S. government to labor groups, environmental organizations and development agencies: the IFC and MIGA are beyond reform. The 50 Years Is Enough Network further demands that the WBG's existing private-sector investments be liquidated to provide funds for reparations to victims of structural adjustment and environmental devastation caused by WBG projects.

IFC and MIGA Are Not Focused on Poverty Alleviation

Rather than make a meaningful effort to target poverty alleviation, the IFC and MIGA operate on the assumption that any economic growth, regardless of its distribution, will help the poor. They pay almost no attention to who actually benefits from the profits that they claim to generate. They support Domino's Pizza in South Africa and cable television in Brazil. They invest in breweries in Romania, Russia, Tanzania and the Czech Republic, expensive private schools in Pakistan and Uganda, and luxury hotels in Egypt, the Maldives, Vanuatu, Costa Rica and Mexico. These projects are sometimes justified on the grounds that they create employment, but if job creation is the goal, there are more effective ways to use limited resources. The institutions have not even devised a way to gauge the relative impact on impoverished peoples of different forms of investment. Roughly two-thirds of the IFC's funding goes to projects in just 15 countries, most of them "middle-income" and thus presumably less in need than other potential clients, but also lower in risk for the invested dollars of the WBG and its private sector partners.

They Mainly Provide Corporate Welfare for Multinationals

The IFC and MIGA's list of clients reads like a "who's who" of transnational corporations. In the past five years MIGA has extended more than $220 million in political risk insurance to support Citibank's global expansion. ExxonMobil, Elf and BP received more than $150 million in support from the IFC and

MIGA during this period. Likewise, $60 million went to Coca-Cola and Pepsi-Cola, $8 million for Kimberly-Klark in China, and more than $13 million to Radisson and Marriott luxury hotels in Costa Rica. The IFC pays lip-service to the importance of small- and medium-sized enterprises that create jobs and reinvest their earnings locally, but the majority of their resources are used to support the expansion of huge corporations into markets that World Bank and World Trade Organization (WTO) policies have forced open.

They Focus on Environmentally Destructive Sectors

At the heart of the IFC-led "Private Sector Development Strategy" is an emphasis on support for the oil, gas, and mining industries. At the end of November 1999, oil and gas projects accounted for 10 percent of the World Bank's portfolio in both Africa and Latin America, roughly 20 percent in East Asia and the Pacific, and even more in Europe and Central Asia. Between 1995 and 1999, the IFC channeled about 15 percent of its money to oil, gas, and mining, and the corresponding figure for MIGA was even higher.

While these institutions claim to be concerned about global warming, they support fossil fuel projects amounting to billions of dollars. By many gauges, the World Bank Group is the leading financier of fossil fuels in the world. The institutions offer only token support for renewable energy efforts.

Their Projects Often Have Disastrous Outcomes

In Chile, the IFC supported the Pangue hydroelectric dam on the Bio-Bio river, but it failed to assess the impact that the project would have on indigenous peoples and the environment. The foundation that was established to support local communities instead became an agent for their resettlement in order to make way for a further dam. The Committee on Human Rights of the American Anthropological Association concluded that there were "numerous violations of human rights [and] environmental values." Similarly, the IFC is currently supporting a Canadian mining corporation in the Kyrgyz Republic. Transporting chemicals to and from the mine has led to three toxic spills in the last two years, the first of which spilled about two tons of cyanide into the Barskoon River. The river is not only a source of drinking water and irrigation for local communities, but is also upstream from the country's largest lake and biggest tourist attraction. The mining company took almost four hours to notify health authorities about the spill. Approximately 2,600 people were treated and more than 1,000 of them were hospitalized.

They Reject the Public's Right to Information

If the way the IFC and MIGA are spending money is not sufficiently outrageous, their denial of basic information to project-affected communities is further evidence of their unaccountable nature. In the case of the Pangue Dam cited above, a Bank-financed independent inspector's report was so damaging that it was censored by the IFC. A subsequent report, authorized by the IFC, was also suppressed and the author was threatened with legal action if he disclosed his findings. Similarly, even after the three toxic spills at the Kyrgyz mine, the IFC refuses to release the "Emergency Spill Response Plan" to local communities. They claim it is a matter of business confidentiality!

IFC and MIGA hide behind information policies that are an insult to those who believe that public institutions should be accountable to the public. They violate U.S. law by failing to make environmental information available at a sufficiently early stage in the project cycle. Reports used by the Board of Directors to judge the merit of a particular project are deemed confidential. Following Board approval, there are no requirements to release any information about the impacts of a project. Environmental and social monitoring reports, emergency response plans, and evaluations are routinely denied to the public.

Time to Take Action!

While IMF and World Bank structural adjustment policies force an end to subsidies for the most basic goods used by the most impoverished people around the world, the IFC continues to offer generous subsidies to huge transnational corporations so they can make profits in middle-income countries. They also offer insurance to corporations against the possibility of governments one day instituting more assertive economic policies (such as nationalization).

Our public institutions should serve higher interests than guaranteeing private profits, particularly when the fate of the most impoverished countries is concerned.

The IMF and Corporate Welfare in Haiti

The U.S. government is a strong supporter of the IMF's involvement in Haiti. The government, and the corporations it represents, have an interest in helping the IMF impose conditions on Haiti.

Haiti is the largest market for U.S. rice in the Caribbean. The IMF program forced Haiti to open up its economy to subsidized rice exports from the United States and to abolish tariff protections on domestic rice. Erly Rice, one of the largest U.S.-based processors and marketers of brand rice products, and its Haitian subsidiary have been the main beneficiaries of these policies. Erly, which imports 40-50 percent of the rice consumed in Haiti, holds a virtual monopoly on rice imports. Because of subsidies to U.S. producers and exporters, and because IMF policies prevent the Haitian government from protecting domestic producers, Erly was able to capture market share in Haiti, displacing local growers.

15

The World Bank's Revolving Door

Charlie Cray

Just weeks after tens of thousands of demonstrators surrounded the World Bank's headquarters in Washington, D.C. to protest the Bank's role in corporate-led globalization, the Bank opened its doors to the first conference of its Staff Exchange Program, or "Share"—a program enabling employee sharing between multinational corporations and the World Bank.

Started by World Bank President James Wolfensohn in 1995, the Share program is, according to Wolfensohn, intended to "foster closer partnerships with external organizations, particularly the private sector, so as to introduce fresh perspectives and new approaches to deliver better services to our clients."

"When Mr. Wolfensohn first came to the Bank, he thought it was much too incestuous in its thinking," states Pauline Ramprasad, Human Resources Manager of the program. "We did things for the clients out there in the developing world, but it was more driven by an internally cloned system of thinking rather than a more open, market-oriented approach."

Wolfensohn won approval from the Bank's board for funding the staff exchange program as well as an executive development program conducted with Harvard and other business schools. "Mr. Wolfensohn's thinking is that there cannot be sustainable development without an active private sector," Ramprasad says.

But critics say the last thing the World Bank needs is closer ties to big business. "I think this Share program is pretty outrageous, because of Wolfensohn's bloated rhetoric about putting smiles on the faces of poor children," says Bruce Rich of the Environmental Defense Fund. "It just shows how he's opened the Bank up like a sieve to all sorts of corporate influence."

The Contractor Connection

Despite Wolfensohn's professed desire to "foster cultural change in the global development community," the "partners" signed onto the Share program are hardly new to the Bank. Dominated by large multinationals, many of the partners are contractors and banks with existing relationships with the World Bank.

The list of the Bank's eighty-five Share partners includes dozens of multinationals, most of which work as Bank contractors or are clients of the Bank's insurance or finance arms. They include: Asea Brown Boveri (ABB), Aventis, BP Amoco, Citibank, Daimler-Chrysler, Deutsche Bank, Dow AgroSciences, Enron, Exxon-Mobil, Nippon Steel, Novartis, Saudi Aramco, Shell and Sumitomo. The few non-corporate partners include related development banks, United Nations agencies, as well as a few nongovernmental organizations, (NGOs) including the World Conservation Union (IUCN) and ActionAid of England.

During the Share conference, the Bank signed on with its eighty-fifth partner—the Samsung Corporation. Currently there are 57 loaned corporate employees and other Share partners working at the Bank, while 40 Bank staffers have worked on assignment outside.

"You'd think their cultures are close enough as it is," says Kenny Bruno, a research associate with the Transnational Resource and Action Center, who has monitored corporate influence at international institutions such as the United Nations. "This just shows the World Bank's true stripes as an organization that adheres to the neoliberal ideology that big business especially can provide the key to sustainability and eliminating poverty."

Even some of the Bank's own partners have expressed surprise at the predominance of multinationals in the program. "In the mid-1980s, I spent two years in the office of the U.K. Executive Director for the World Bank, so I expected to fit in pretty easily when I came to the World Bank in September 1999," says Gregory Toulmin of the British Government's Department for International Development in Share's first newsletter. "In fact I suffered several shocks, starting with the very private sector oriented nature of the staff exchange."

Asked why the program is dominated by relationships with multinationals, Ramprasad says, "we're working to balance that out. For instance, we want to involve more of the emerging private sector from places like Africa, and while the emphasis continues heavily to be on the private sector, we now have regional development banks, specialized UN agencies, and so on. We also have NGOs and even a couple of ministries of finance."

Bank officials claim the exchange program ensures there are also no conflicts of interest despite the fact that there is no policy restricting the exchange of staff while a company is bidding on Bank projects. Once seconded to the Bank, the new partners are not allowed to work on anything related to their parent company. "We rigorously manage even the perception of conflicts of interest," says Ramprasad. "Everyone at the Bank has to agree to its conflict of interest policy, which doesn't stop when you leave the Bank. It continues a couple of years after that."

Nevertheless, when asked what the corporations get from the program, Ramprasad says, "they get a lot out of it. For one, if the private sector is thinking of how to establish business in a country, with the Bank they're involved with the country policy dialogue. This could, as a by-product, help them understand how the Bank operates and why the Bank would make certain policy decisions about loans which they may bid on at a later date...just because you're working with us you get an advantage by knowing how to do that."

Bank officials claim they have learned many of the efficiencies and "line-oriented results" of business culture. Most important, apparently, is the Bank's ability to learn from its partners how to effectively implement marketization plans, e.g. privatization of public services, including water and electricity.

Long-Term Trend

Bank-corporate staff exchange is not novel in the agricultural sector. The agrochemical industry including multinationals such as Dow, Aventis, and Rhone Poulenc—have had a long history of placing staff at the World Bank. Now these staff exchanges are conducted through the Share program. "In a sense the Share program is nothing new," says Bruce Rich. "It's a very insider practice."

Asked how pesticide companies help the Bank live up to specific commitments such as improving its work on Integrated Pest Management (IPM), Ramprasad says specific concerns such as this are best left to the Bank's rural development unit. "They have constant discussions back and forth with the private sector and the farmers," she says. "We've got people from Aventis and Rhone Poulenc, too."

Yet NGOs monitoring the Bank's agricultural policies believe the staff exchange program should do more to reflect the Bank's stated policy objectives, including those which address environmental sustainability. "Partnerships with pesticide companies create a major conflict of interest and undermine the credibility of the World Bank's stated commitment to funding purchases of chemical pesticides only as a last resort," says Jessica Hamburger, a project coordinator with Pesticide Action Network North America.

Converging Cultures

World Bank energy planners who have participated in the Share program appear to be affected by a kind of creep towards corporate culture. Jayme Porto Carreiro, a Bank Senior Energy Planner, describes his experience at Electricité de France, where "I was to drop everything and manage the purchase of London

Electricity, a large power distribution company in England." Facing a need to get approval from the EU's competition commission, "my experience as Bank staff proved invaluable. I did what any of my colleagues would have done. I instructed the lawyers to tell the European Commission to change its laws. I won't pretend it was easy, but we did persuade the EU to do just that—moreover, to do it in less than a month."

Despite conflict of interest rules, once seconded to a multinational, Bank officials are free to put their experience to work in the company's interest. As Donald O'Leary, a senior power engineer at the World Bank, explains, "because of my experience working on dam projects for the World Bank, Siemens AG nominated me to support the work of the World Commission on Dams as part of my responsibilities in Germany. My involvement in the Commission's activities have taught me that its work is unique.... The Commission membership was carefully balanced to represent all sides of the dams debate."

NGO watchdogs question if Bank officials are clear about what "side" they represent once they return to the Bank from such an experience. "The main problem is the kind of incestuous thinking this program perpetuates," says Patrick McCully of the International Rivers Network. "They'll inevitably be thinking of projects that include contracts that companies like Siemens and Electricité de France want to bid on, and technological solutions that only the multinationals are into. Smaller scale ways of generating electricity or reducing demand are going to be less attractive."

Some of the Share program's partners are involved in many of the most controversial projects on the Bank's docket. For instance, ExxonMobil is the leader of a consortium seeking Bank approval for a major pipeline in Chad and Cameroon and Electricité de France is a major player in the Nam Theun 2 dam proposed for Laos.

Critics' complaints notwithstanding, Bank officials say they have seen the future, and Share is at its center. "In the end, the almost five billion people who live in emerging economies deserve the benefits that an effective global development partnership can provide," says Wolfensohn.

Because the World Bank (1) functions as a partner with multinational corporations through its International Finance Corporation, (2) pushes for an expanded role for the private sector through its structural and sectoral adjustment loans, and (3) generally blurs the public-private sector distinction, perhaps it should be no surprise that the distinction is becoming hazy even when it comes to Bank staffing.

Chixoy Dam Reparations Campaign

In 1954, the U.S. government orchestrated the violent overthrow of a democratically elected Guatemalan government. Until the late 1990s, Guatemala was ruled by the military. During this time, the Guatemalan regime was funded, trained, armed and otherwise supported by Washington. During the worst repression, the World Bank helped fund the construction of the Chixoy hydroelectric dam in Rabinal, Guatemala. The projected flood basin of the Chixoy Dam was inhabited by Mayan Achi communities that had lived there for centuries.

The village of Rio Negro was opposed to the construction of the dam. In large part as a result of their peaceful opposition to the project, more than 440 community members were murdered by Guatemalan security forces. The filling of the dam basin began in January 1983, shortly after the final massacre in September 1982. After the massacres and filling of the Chixoy dam basin, the World Bank gave further loans to Guatemala to complete the project.

For information on the campaign for reparations to be paid to the people of Guatemala, see www.rightsaction.org.

16

Silencing Joseph Stiglitz

David Moberg

After World Bank chief economist Joseph Stiglitz quit his job in November 1999 in order to speak more openly about his disagreements with policies of the Bank and the International Monetary Fund, the World Bank still retained the distinguished economist as a special advisor to president James D. Wolfensohn. But Stiglitz's criticism finally proved too much for the powerful global financial institutions, especially after they endured raucous protests in April 2000 at their spring meetings. In May, even as he was traveling to drought-stricken Ethiopia on a Bank mission and his replacement had not yet taken office, the World Bank announced that he would no longer serve as special advisor.

Defenders of the IMF and World Bank can denigrate the credentials of some protesters, but it is hard to attack the widely published former Stanford professor who also served as chairman of President Clinton's Council of Economic Advisors. His candor made him an unlikely intellectual guru to the world trade protest movement. But while his criticism enhanced the credibility of the protesters, it also prompted new pressure to quiet him, even as the global financial institutions were promising critics they would be more open and transparent.

During his tenure at the World Bank, Stiglitz irritated many powerful colleagues by publicly criticizing IMF moves and calling for more open debate about global economic policies. Until recently the World Bank and IMF had presented a united front to the world as they tried to solve global economic problems. Often the IMF has helped troubled countries which hold loans from World Bank funds that are tied to agreements by those countries to take the IMF cure: cutting government budgets and subsidies; privatizing public operations; raising interest rates; opening national economies to foreign imports, corporations and capital; and increasing exports of raw materials or goods made with labor made even cheaper by these policies.

These policy packages made up the "Washington consensus" imposed by the IMF with World Bank support for more than two decades—despite an unimpressive track record on nearly every count except reducing inflation and budget deficits. When Stiglitz announced last year that he was leaving the bank and returning to academic life, there were rumors that he was pushed out because he was too outspoken. "Pushed out would not be the way I'd put it," he said, "But it was made very clear...the way I put it was that whenever you have institutional responsibilities, you have less freedom to express yourself, especially clearly and forcefully. Part of the culture within the institution and within finance ministries is that the two institutions should not criticize each other."

The mass protests in mid-April 2000, which Stiglitz thought were "quite successful", "challenged that pact of silence." Some news media coverage of the protests "focused on the broader message: that what is at issue is a question of values, of democratic processes, and how, partly because of the absence of democratic process, decisions were made that jeopardized the livelihoods and even the lives of many of the world's poor."

"Unfortunately," he said, the Bank and IMF did not have a "totally positive" response and became defensive and even less open, as Stiglitz's removal confirms. "There was certainly no engagement on the broad fundamental question about democratic process and whether there was a balance of representation in the decision-making process—of financial interests versus workers," Stiglitz said. "What's remarkable, I see no indication of a grasp of that even as an issue. A reaction one heard within the organization was very much that 'They're impugning our motives.'" Both organizations are accustomed to impugning motives of governments and analyzing how incentives and interests drive other people and institutions, but they "feel very uncomfortable when that light is shined on them," Stiglitz said.

We know that IMF and World Bank programs have greatly exacerbated poverty and undermined the basic human and democratic rights of people in Southern countries to determine our own destiny. This is why we support a campaign of the boycott of World Bank bonds. Some 80 percent of the World Banks' capital—money that it uses to enforce structural adjustment, privatization, increasing user fees for education and health care, and projects which destroy poor people's lives in the name of progress—come from private capital markets and not from governments. Churches, universities, and trade unions which hold these bonds in their investments are subsidizing an institution which is the enemy of human freedom, just as institutions which held stock in companies doing business with the Apartheid regime supported the ability of the Apartheid regime to remain in power. By challenging public institutions to commit NOT to buy World Bank Bonds, we will give students, church groups, and trade union activists a means to pressure these institutions...

Dennis Brutus, Jubilee 2000 South Africa, "A campaign to Break the Power of the World Bank", Letter to South African Colleagues [September 10, 1999]

17

Collateral Damage at the World Bank

Nicola Bullard

The reputation of the World Bank was struck another blow in mid-2000, following news that Dr. Ravi Kanbur, team leader and principal author of this year's *World Development Report*, had resigned in protest at attempts by the U.S. Treasury Department to 'water down' his message.

While Kanbur's resignation did not become public until June 14, the events that forced his departure occurred several weeks earlier when the draft *World Development Report* was presented to the Bank's board of directors. At this meeting, both the Bank's president James Wolfensohn and its managing director Jeff Goldstein (recruited for the job from Wolfensohn's old investment firm on Wall Street) pushed for more emphasis on 'growth' as opposed to 'poverty reduction.' Soon after, on May 23, there was a meeting between Kanbur and Goldstein (and possibly some U.S. Treasury officials). After the meeting Kanbur went home and didn't return to the Bank. He resigned on May 25.

Kanbur's exit followed hard on the heels of former chief economist Joseph Stiglitz's premature departure. It seems that the Bank, despite it's re-packaging as a 'listening' institution, is having difficulty listening to its senior staff, especially when they express views that deviate even slightly from the hard-line "Growth is Good" faction inside and outside the Bank.

Bank on the Ropes

The World Bank is in crisis, partly of its own making and partly because of the particular constellation of political events swirling around it.

The debate on the Meltzer Commission's recommendations to significantly downsize both the Bank and the IMF reached a stalemate in Congress. Treasury Secretary Larry Summers— speaking for the Clinton administration—rejected the commission's proposals saying that they would "weaken the IMF, the World Bank and other regional development banks to the point where vital U.S. interests would be compromised because of the reduction in their capacity to respond effectively to promote market-oriented development in the world."

You have to admit, there's something about Larry. His frankness is disarming and his shameless pairing of U.S. interests and market-oriented development leaves no room for doubt about where the administration sees its interests.

On the other, the Republicans don't like either the IMF or the World Bank for a ragbag of reasons (everything from being tainted by the same lefty brush as the U.N. to interfering in the free market) and the Meltzer recommendations tally well with their neo-isolationist tendencies. And it seems they are willing to block budget appropriations for debt relief and AIDS programs in the Third World (both dear to the Democrats' bleeding heart) to force concessions from the Democrats.

So the equation was something like this: Both the Bank and Summers wanted to close the Meltzer debate before the November 2000 elections because they knew that a Republican administration would be much more sympathetic to the commission's proposals and might even mount a full-scale assault on the Bank. The Democrats wanted to squeeze the last drop of political mileage out of the system to increase their own electoral chances, and if this meant striking a deal with the Republicans to get through some more populist budget items, they might just do it. And of course the Republicans were feeling confident that George

"Dubya" Bush would be in the Oval Office in January and could probably hold the line on Meltzer until the terms are right. Murky waters indeed, but all relevant to what has been going on at the Bank in recent months.

Powerful Friends Are Better Than Ideas

There is no doubt that Wolfensohn must be worried about what a Republican administration would do to the Bank. After all, he's got almost another five years to go and he doesn't want to spend it at the helm of a sinking ship. To keep the ship afloat he has to walk the line between two major constituencies. The first are the critics (and even though Wolfensohn may feel personally "betrayed" by the April 16 protests after all he had done to "open the Bank and listen to his critics," they will not go away).

The second is the U.S. Treasury Department. You don't need to be a World Bank economist to do the cost benefit analysis. To save the Bank, and his own reputation—Wolfensohn has always approached his work at the Bank as a personal 'mission' or in his words 'the work of God'—it is essential that the Bank's policies and public pronouncements do not stray too far from its main shareholder and political protector, the U.S. Treasury Department. While Treasury Secretary Larry Summers must also be wondering about his post-election future and counting his friends in Congress, he also knows first-hand that tame multilateral institutions give the United States foreign policy and economic leverage on the cheap, something which the isolationist Republicans do not fully understand. And Summers has his own history in the Bank, and no doubt wants to preserve his intellectual heritage: exemplified by his now legendary memo on the impeccable market logic of dumping toxic waste in the Third World. (See page 115.) Pretenders to the throne, and especially those who want to introduce heretical ideas such as redistribution, need to be brought into line.

The issue at the heart of the debate is growth versus poverty reduction. In this sense, Kanbur's challenge to the system is far greater than that of Stiglitz. Although Stiglitz did stir up the system, he also believed in the benefits of an open and globalized economy. What he argued was that the market on its own cannot achieve this and so it is necessary to include non-economic factors such as social capital, participation and democracy.

Kanbur's reported emphasis on 'empowerment' (code for redistribution) is a much more lethal attack on the orthodoxy. And of course, translating this into the U.S. context we can understand why Summers is so nervous: the growth figures for the U.S. are impressive, but the cleavages between rich and poor are deepening. The U.S. cannot afford to support a critique of growth and globalization that would have such dramatic implications for its own economic policies.

According to Larry Summers, "discussions of poverty reduction that do not lay primary emphasis on economic growth are like Hamlet without the prince." Perhaps the analogy is better than Summers imagines if we recall the story of Hamlet. The setting is Elsinore (Washington, or the World Bank perhaps) a hotbed of political plotting, steeped in corruption and intrigue. The Good King is murdered by his conniving wife and friend, while the hero, Prince Hamlet, stalks the ramparts, talking to ghosts, growing more paranoid, and eventually succumbing to his own delusions. As the hero said, there is something rotten in the state of Denmark.

All over Africa, the demand for democratic ownership and control of our economies has formed a central pillar of our struggle for national liberation. It is this legacy of struggle and resistance that we are building upon in our present struggle against...IMF-World Bank structural adjustment.

> Declaration of the African Delegation at the
> International Meeting, "The Dictatorship of
> Financial Markets: Another World is Possible,"
> Paris, June 24-26, 1999

18

Bank Chief and Bishops Clash

Madeleine Bunting

The President of the World Bank angrily defended his organization's record on Third World debt before 735 Anglican bishops. Addressing the Lambeth, England world conference in late 1999, including the Archbishop of Canterbury, James Wolfensohn called on the Church to stop fighting him and work with him to alleviate poverty.

Reacting to attacks by Christian Aid, Wolfensohn warned the bishops: "We have expertise on development, you have expertise in people and in communities. You have the biggest distribution system of any non-governmental organization in the world. We can service the poor better together. Instead of fighting each other, we can work together."

His outburst followed the voicing of almost unanimous outrage by the bishops at the meeting in Canterbury at the cost in human suffering of spiraling debt in the Third World. After a tense week of controversy over the issue of homosexuality, most declared world debt the most important item at the conference.

The Archbishop of Canterbury, Dr. George Carey, said international debt was a moral issue and Christian churches had a crucial role in tackling global injustice. He said: "The depths of suffering which we continue to see in many parts of that great continent (Africa) go far beyond what is tolerable in a civilized world. The churches have a key role in creating the climate for change. It is a moral problem of enormous proportions."

Many of the bishops are members of the Jubilee 2000 campaign for the cancellation of unpayable debt. Archbishop of Cape Town, Njongonkulu Ndungane, said: "We live in the grip of an economy which encourages overlending and overborrowing. But the poorest are not just in the grip of this economy, they are enslaved by it. For every $1 that rich countries send to developing countries, $11 comes straight back in the form of repayment on debts owed to the richest countries. This is a form of economics that denies us our humanity, rich and poor alike."

Pope Warns Against Globalization

Pope John Paul II, in a May Day 2000 mass for workers from around the world, said that globalization of investment and trade should not be allowed to violate basic human rights. The pope, who later that day made an appeal for cancelling Third World debt, said humanity should see the new millennium as an opportunity to rediscover the authentic value of work. "It invites us to face the economic and social imbalances that exist in the world of work and re-establish a correct hierarchy of values, where the dignity of men and women who work, their freedom, responsibility and participation assume the top priority," he said.

Addressing a crowd including Juan Somavia, director-general of the International Labor Organization, and delegations of workers from 54 countries, the pope said high technology should not lead to low values. "New realities which are forcefully affecting the productive process, such as globalization of finance, of the economy, of commerce and of work, should never be allowed to violate the dignity and centrality of the human person or the democracy of peoples," he said.

The pope expressed particular concern for the unemployed, underemployed and under-paid. "I feel very close in spirit to people who are forced to live in a poverty which offends their dignity and blocks them from sharing the goods of the earth and forcing them to feed themselves with what falls from the table of the rich," he said.

Section Three:

Where Does the Movement Go From Here?

This section raises, and attempts to answer, key questions about how the movement for change can further weaken the World Bank and the IMF, and replace them with more humane, democratic, and ecological institutions. The articles in this section also raise larger questions about the transition from a profit-driven global economy controlled by the few. to a sustainable, democratic model predicated on human rights and saving the environment.

In "A Brief History of Resistance to Structural Adjustment," George Caffentzis and Silvia Federici show that the protests in Washington against the World Bank and the IMF were preceded by a rich legacy of third world resistance.

Naomi Klein's "The Vision Thing" explores the strengths and weaknesses of the movement for global economic justice and defends the movement against critics who hear the diverse voices but fail to see the unifying organizational structure and ideology.

"Baby Steps to a Global Revolution?" is an interview with Juliette Beck, one of the rising young leaders of the movement for a democratic global economy.

In "Defunding the Fund, Running on the Bank," Patrick Bond celebrates what he sees as an incipient movement against global capitalism, yet he warns protesters that they need to deepen their theoretical understanding of what they are protesting.

In "Structural Adjustment is Hitting the U.S. Too," Anuradha Mittal makes the connections between policies recently imposed on people in the United States with similar policies that have been forced on third world debtor countries for decades.

The 50 Years Is Enough Network ("Demands for Transforming the World Bank and the IMF") has taken the lead in laying out the details of how the Bank and IMF must be transformed in order to satisfy a movement whose political center of gravity is shifting from a reformist position to an abolitionist position.

"Boycotting World Bank Bonds" by Neil Watkins and Kevin Danaher lays out why and how to build a movement to hit the World Bank where it hurts—at their main source of revenue.

Kevin Danaher ("An Alternative to the Debt Crisis") offers a proposal for a way the internationalist movement could impose mass democratic conditionality on elites and transfer debt relief money down to grassroots organizations.

Deborah James concludes the section ("Twelve Ways to Democratize the U.S. Political Sytem") with specific ways we can help democratize the global economy by breaking the corporate stranglehold on the U.S. system of governance.

Despite years of relative peace and prosperity in industrialized countries, global poverty is getting worse. Some 1.2 billion people now live in extreme poverty. More troubling still is the massive and widening gap between rich and poor. In Brazil, for example, the poorest 20 percent of the population earn just 2.5 percent of the country's income, and the richest 20 percent control nearly two-thirds. This is not just an extreme case. Alarming ratios are seen in countries as different as Colombia and Niger, South Africa and Russia. This cannot go on indefinitely without a backlash.

James D. Wolfensohn,
President of the World Bank

19

A Brief History of Resistance to Structural Adjustment

George Caffentzis and Silvia Federici

I n the dozens of countries where the International Monetary Fund and World Bank have imposed Structural Adjustment Programs (SAPs), people have not been passive when they experience deterioration in their standards of living, reduced access to public services, devastated environments, and plummeting employment prospects. The pages of newspapers, magazines, and academic journals (those that can survive in depressed economies) have been filled with damning analysis of structural adjustment. More importantly, people have been organizing to combat the pillaging of their lands and livelihoods. This organizing has resulted in mass movements and protests on every continent, but they are not often reported in the mainstream press. A selection of notable struggles in the last 20 years of fighting structural adjustment follows.

ALGERIA
October 1988: More than 200 people are killed in rioting against high prices and unemployment in wake of SAP.

BENIN
January-June 1989: Students at the University of Cotonou go

on strike, paralyzing the institution for six months, in protest of nonpayment of grants for several months and the government's intention to stop paying them altogether in 1989 as part of SAP reforms. Teachers strike begins in April, with demands for payment of four months' salary arrears, the withdrawal of the 50 percent reduction in their salaries (part of IMF mandates), the unconditional liberation of all teachers, pupils, and students held during the strike and the reintegration of 401 teachers dismissed in March for striking.

BOLIVIA

March 1985: A general strike is called by labor unions, with the support of many agricultural workers, against government's sharp increase in food and gasoline prices as part of its IMF-designed SAP. Troops and riot police are called out. Unions accept government's offer to increase basic minimum wage by more than four-fold along with other wage increases.

April 2000: Mass protests against World Bank-inspired plans by the Bolivian government to privatize water supplies; at least seven protesters are killed by police. Government eventually backs down on privatization plan.

September-October 2000: Widespread rebellion by small farmers—who feel the government is corrupt and is ignoring the rural population—is met by government repression: more than ten people are killed and dozens are wounded by police and military. Government of President Hugo Banzer eventually makes concessions in an attempt to quell the persistent rebellion.

ECUADOR

March 1987: Students in Quito clash with riot policemen during protests against government's SAP.

October 1987: Workers in Ecuador firebomb a bank and block streets with tires during one-day general strike against SAP.

June-August 1999: A broad coalition of civil society organizations, led by indigenous peasants, rise up to demand the curtailment of austerity measures imposed after the IMF's emergency interventions in the wake of weather catastrophes, further destabilizing the government.

January 2000: Indigenous people march on Quito to demand an end to austerity programs and more responsive government. After taking over the parliament building and allying with key members of the military, the indigenous organizations succeed in forcing the resignation of President Jamil Mahuad. Betrayal by the head of the armed forces leads to the vice-president taking over leadership rather than a government of national reconciliation.

JAMAICA

January 1985: Demonstrators across the country protest the government's decision to raise fuel prices in accordance with an SAP that began with a 1982 World Bank loan that was renegotiated in November 1984.

JORDAN

April 1989: Riots over increased food prices erupt throughout southern Jordan shortly after announcement of SAP agreed to with IMF. At least five protesters are killed by police.

August 1996: Riots break out in Karak and other southern cities after IMF demands removal of subsidies, resulting in tripling of price of bread. King suspends Parliament when it refuses to support price hikes. Protesters also target Ministry of Education because of hike in school fees connected with IMF program.

MEXICO

January 1994: Zapatista Army of National Liberation begins insurrection against NAFTA and SAP-style policies of the PRI government. The insurrection destabilizes the government and these policies.

NIGER

February 1990: Students at University of Niamey boycott classes to protest adoption of reductions in educational funding mandated by SAP. During the course of a peaceful demonstration police fire on demonstrators killing three (according to official police sources) or 14 (according to student leaders). Many others are wounded.

NIGERIA

May 1986: Roughly twenty students and bystanders at Ahmadu Bello University (ABU) in Zaria are massacred by security forces after staging peaceful protests over impending introduction of SAP. More students are killed in protests against SAP and the ABU massacre during the following days at Kaduna Polytechnic, the University of Benin, and the University of Lagos.

April 1988: Students demonstrate at 33 universities against fuel price increase demanded by IMF-inspired SAP.

May-June 1989: Dozens of people are killed and hundreds are arrested in riots and strikes against SAP in Lagos, Benin City, and Port Harcourt. Government is forced to offer a welfare program called an "SAP Relief Package," the establishment of a mass transit scheme and a "People's Bank," and a review of the minimum wage.

March-May 1990: Students and faculty on campuses nationwide protest government's decision to accept a $150 million university restructuring loan from the World Bank, especially conditions requiring closure of many departments and programs. The military government stages armed assaults and hundreds of arrests, with hundreds more expelled from the university system.

May 1992: Students at Universities of Ibadan and Lagos protest against implementation of SAP, which they accuse of being responsible for the deterioration of campus facilities and education programs as well as the doubling of transport prices. Police respond by shooting demonstrators, wounding at least five. Battles between young antigovernment demonstrators and police in Lagos leave at least three dead and hundreds injured. The IMF and World Bank made the removal of subsidies and probable increase of the price of gasoline the main imperative in its negotiations with the Nigerian government.

PARAGUAY

June 1999: A 48-hour general strike is called on June 22 in response to the government's plans to privatize its telephone, water, and railroad companies. The privatizations are conditions of an IMF program that Paraguay must meet in order to access $400 million in World Bank loans. Police meet the protesters with violence almost immediately, resulting in 20 injuries and at least 10 arrests. About 300 protesters in Fernando de la Mora are dispersed by police with water cannons.

RUSSIA

December 1993: Coalition of parties opposed to the neoliberal reform (SAP) measures of the Yeltsin government win a majority in parliamentary elections.

SUDAN

October-November 1987: Steep currency devaluation and price hikes resulting from arrangements with both the IMF and World Bank lead to demonstrations by about 15,000 in Khartoum to denounce the IMF. Students at the University of Khartoum occupy buildings, leading to eventual closure of the institution. Street violence and arrests follow.

TRINIDAD

July 28-August 2, 1990: The Society of Muslims assaults government headquarters and takes President Robinson and other members of the cabinet hostage, demanding an end to IMF-imposed economic austerity measures. Riots and looting follow the assault in Port of Spain; at least 50 people are killed.

UGANDA

December 1990: Students at Makerere University protest the government for cutting stationery and travel allowances arising from a World Bank-imposed SAP. Police fire into a crowd of protesting students, killing two.

VENEZUELA

February 28-March 2, 1989: About 600 people are killed and more than 1,000 are wounded in rioting over economic measures, including sharp increases in fuel and public transport prices, imposed to satisfy the IMF and World Bank. President Perez, as one of his first acts in office, signed a letter of intent with the IMF putting into place an SAP on February 23.

February 1992: Coup attempt by middle-level military officers—widely supported by the population—fails. The economic goal of the coup's protagonists was the end of Venezuela's SAP. Leader of the coup attempt, Hugo Chavez, is elected President in 1999.

ZAIRE (now DEMOCRATIC REPUBLIC OF CONGO)

March 1985: Students at Mbanza Ngungu and Mbuji Mai Universities criticize cuts in higher education budget adopted by the government in compliance with IMF's SAP.

ZAMBIA

January-February 1987: Food price riots in the northern copper mining district in response to an SAP announced in December 1986 eventually lead to program's suspension.

A September 2000 report by the World Development Movement (U.K.), *States of Unrest: Resistance to IMF Policies in Poor Countries,* reveals that since the Seattle protests of November 30, 1999, there have been at least 50 separate episodes of civil unrest in 13 poor countries, all directed at the IMF. Half of these have ended in violent clashes with the police or military. For the full report, visit WDM's website (www.wdm.org.uk).

20

The Vision Thing:
Are The Protests Unfocused, Or Are Critics Missing The Point?

Naomi Klein

This conference is not like other conferences." That's what all the speakers at "Re-Imagining Politics and Society" were told before we arrived at New York's Riverside Church. When we addressed the delegates (there were about 1,000, over three days in May 2000), we were to try to solve a very specific problem: the lack of "unity of vision and strategy" guiding the movement against global corporatism.

This was a very serious problem, we were advised. The young activists who went to Seattle to shut down the World Trade Organization and to Washington, D.C., to protest the World Bank and the IMF had been getting hammered in the press as tree-wearing, lamb-costumed, drumbeating bubble brains. Our mission, according to the conference organizers at the Foundation for Ethics and Meaning, was to whip that chaos on the streets into some kind of structured, media-friendly shape. This wasn't just another talk shop. We were going to "give birth to a unified movement for holistic social, economic, and political change."

As I slipped in and out of lecture rooms, soaking up vision from Arianna Huffington, Michael Lerner, David Korten, and Cornel West, I was struck by the futility of this entire well-meaning exercise. Even if we did manage to come up with a ten-point plan—brilliant in its clarity, elegant in its coherence, unified in its outlook—to whom, exactly, would we hand down these commandments? The anticorporate protest movement that came to world attention on the streets of Seattle in November 1999 is not united by a political party or a national network with a head office, annual elections, and subordinate cells and locals. It is shaped by the ideas of individual organizers and intellectuals, but doesn't defer to any of them as leaders. In this amorphous context, the ideas and plans being hatched at the Riverside Church weren't irrelevant exactly, they just weren't important in the way they clearly hoped to be. Rather than changing the world, they were destined to be swept up and tossed around in the tidal wave of information—web diaries, NGO manifestos, academic papers, homemade videos, *cris de coeur*—that the global anticorporate network produces and consumes each and every day.

This is the flip side of the persistent criticism that the kids on the street lack clear leadership—they lack clear followers too. To those searching for replicas of the 1960s, this absence makes the anticorporate movement appear infuriatingly impassive. Evidently, these people are so disorganized they can't even get it together to respond to perfectly well-organized efforts to organize them. These are MTV-weaned activists, you can practically hear the old guard saying: scattered, nonlinear, no focus.

It's easy to be persuaded by these critiques. If there is one thing on which the left and right agree, it is the value of a clear, well-structured ideological argument. But maybe it's not quite so simple. Maybe the protests in Seattle and Washington look unfocused because they were not demonstrations of one movement at all but rather convergences of many smaller ones, each with its sights trained on a specific multinational corporation (like Nike), a particular industry (like agribusiness), or a new trade initiative (like the Free Trade Area of the Americas). These smaller, targeted movements are clearly part of a common cause: They share a belief that the disparate problems with which they are wrestling all derive from global deregulation, an agenda that is concentrating power and wealth into fewer and fewer hands.

Of course, there are disagreements: about the role of the nation-state, about whether capitalism is redeemable, about the speed with which change should occur. But within most of these miniature movements, there is an emerging consensus that building community-based decision-making power—whether through unions, neighborhoods, farms, villages, anarchist collectives, or aboriginal self-government—is essential to countering the might of multinational corporations.

Despite this common ground, these campaigns have not coalesced into a single movement. Rather, they are intricately and tightly linked to one another, much as "hotlinks" connect their websites on the Internet. This analogy is more than coincidental and is in fact key to understanding the changing nature of political organizing. Although many have observed that the recent mass protests would have been impossible without the Internet, what has been overlooked is how the communication technology that facilitates these campaigns is shaping the movement in its own image. Thanks to the Net, mobilizations are able to unfold with sparse bureaucracy and minimal hierarchy; forced consensus and labored manifestos are fading into the background, replaced instead by a culture of constant, loosely structured and sometimes compulsive information-swapping.

What emerged on the streets of Seattle and Washington was an activist model that mirrors the organic, decentralized, interlinked pathways of the Internet—the Internet come to life.

The Washington-based research center TeleGeography has taken it upon itself to map out the architecture of the Internet as if it were the solar system. Recently, TeleGeography pronounced that the Internet is not one giant web but a network of "hubs and spokes." The hubs are the centers of activity, the spokes the links to other centers, which are autonomous but interconnected.

It seems like a perfect description of the protests in Seattle and Washington, D.C. These mass convergences were activist hubs, made up of hundreds, possibly thousands, of autonomous spokes. During the demonstrations, the spokes took the form of "affinity groups" of between five and twenty protesters, each of which elected a spokesperson to represent them at regular "spokescouncil" meetings. Although the affinity groups agreed to abide by a set of nonviolence principles, they also functioned as discrete units, with the power to make their own strategic decisions. At some rallies, activists carry actual cloth webs to symbolize their movement. When it's time for a meeting, they lay the web on the ground, call out "all spokes on the web" and the structure becomes a street-level boardroom.

In the four years before the Seattle and Washington protests, similar hub events had converged outside WTO, G-7, and Asia Pacific Economic Cooperation summits in Auckland, Vancouver, Manila, Birmingham, London, Geneva, Kuala Lumpur, and Cologne. These mass protests were organized according to principles of coordinated decentralization. Rather than present a coherent front, small units of activists surrounded their target from all directions. And rather than build elaborate national or international bureaucracies, temporary structures were thrown up instead: Empty buildings were turned into "Convergence Centers," and independent media producers assembled impromptu activist news centers. The *ad hoc* coalitions behind these demonstrations frequently named themselves after the date of the planned event: J18, N30, A16, S26. When these events are over, they leave virtually no trace behind, save for an archived website.

Of course, all this talk of radical decentralization conceals a very real hierarchy based on who owns, understands, and controls the computer networks linking the activists to one another— this is what Jesse Hirsh, one of the founders of the anarchist computer network Tao Communications, calls "a geek adhocracy."

The hubs and spokes model is more than a tactic used at protests; the protests are themselves made up of "coalitions of coalitions," to borrow a phrase from Kevin Danaher of Global Exchange. Each anti-corporate campaign is made up of many groups, mostly NGOs, labor unions, students and anarchists. They use the Internet, as well as more traditional organizing tools, to do everything from cataloguing the latest transgressions of the World Bank to bombarding Shell Oil with faxes and e-mails to distributing ready-to-download anti-sweatshop leaflets for protests at Nike Town. The groups remain autonomous, but their international coordination is deft and, to their targets, frequently devastating.

The charge that the anticorporate movement lacks "vision" falls apart when looked at in the context of these campaigns. It's true that the mass protests in Seattle and D.C. were a hodgepodge of slogans and causes, that to a casual observer, it was hard to decode the connections between Mumia's incarceration and the fate of the sea turtles. But in trying to find coherence in these large-scale shows of strength, the critics are confusing the outward demonstrations of the movement with the thing itself— missing the forest for the people dressed as trees. This movement is its spokes, and in the spokes there is no shortage of vision.

The student anti-sweatshop movement, for instance, has rapidly moved from simply criticizing companies and campus administrators to drafting alternate codes of conduct and building its own quasi-regulatory body, the Worker Rights Consortium. The movement against genetically engineered and modified foods has leapt from one policy victory to the next, first getting many genetically modified foods removed from the shelves of British supermarkets, then getting labeling laws passed in Europe, then making enormous strides with the Montreal Protocol on Biosafety. Meanwhile, opponents of the World Bank's and IMF's export-led development models have produced bookshelves' worth of resources on community-based development models, debt relief, and self-government principles. Critics of the oil and mining industries are similarly overflowing with ideas for sustainable energy and responsible resource extraction—though they rarely get the chance to put their visions into practice.

The fact that these campaigns are so decentralized is not a

source of incoherence and fragmentation. Rather, it is a reasonable, even ingenious adaptation both to pre-existing fragmentation within progressive networks and to changes in the broader culture. It is a by-product of the explosion of NGOs, which, since the Rio Summit in 1992, have been gaining power and prominence. There are so many NGOs involved in anticorporate campaigns that nothing but the hubs and spokes model could possibly accommodate all their different styles, tactics, and goals. Like the Internet itself, both the NGO and the affinity group networks are infinitely expandable systems. If somebody doesn't feel like they quite fit in to one of the 30,000 or so NGOs or thousands of affinity groups out there, they can just start their own and link up. Once involved, no one has to give up their individuality to the larger structure; as with all things on-line, we are free to dip in and out, take what we want and delete what we don't. It is a surfer's approach to activism reflecting the Internet's paradoxical culture of extreme narcissism coupled with an intense desire for external connection.

One of the great strengths of this model of laissez-faire organizing is that it has proven extraordinarily difficult to control, largely because it is so different from the organizing principles of the institutions and corporations it targets. It responds to corporate concentration with a maze of fragmentation, to globalization with its own kind of localization, to power consolidation with radical power dispersal.

Joshua Karliner of the Transnational Resource and Action Center calls this system "an unintentionally brilliant response to globalization." And because it was unintentional, we still lack even the vocabulary to describe it, which may be why a rather amusing metaphor industry has evolved to fill the gap. I'm throwing my lot in with hubs and spokes, but Maude Barlow of the Council of Canadians says, "We are up against a boulder. We can't remove it so we try to go underneath it, to go around it, and over it." Britain's John Jordan, one of the founders of Reclaim the Streets, says transnationals "are like giant tankers, and we

are like a school of fish. We can respond quickly; they can't."
The U.S.-based Free Burma Coalition talks of a network of "spiders," spinning a web strong enough to tie down the most powerful multinationals. A U.S. military report about the Zapatista uprising in Chiapas even got in on the game. According to a study produced by the RAND Corporation, the Zapatistas were waging "a war of the flea" that, thanks to the Internet and the global NGO network, turned into a "war of the swarm." The military challenge of a war of the swarm, the researchers noted, is that it has no "central leadership or command structure; it is multiheaded, impossible to decapitate."

Of course, this multiheaded system has its weaknesses too, and they were on full display on the streets of Washington during the anti-World Bank/IMF protests. At around noon on April 16, the day of the largest protest, a spokescouncil meeting was convened for the affinity groups that were in the midst of blocking all the street intersections surrounding the headquarters of the World Bank and the IMF. The intersections had been blocked since 6:00 A.M., but the meeting delegates, the protesters had just learned, had slipped inside the police barricades before 5:00 A.M. Given this new information, most of the spokespeople felt it was time to give up the intersections and join the official march at the Ellipse. The problem was that not everyone agreed: A handful of affinity groups wanted to see if they could block the delegates on their way out of their meetings.

The compromise the council came up with was telling. "OK, everybody listen up," Kevin Danaher shouted into a megaphone. "Each intersection has autonomy. If the intersection wants to stay locked down, that's cool. If it wants to come to the Ellipse, that's cool too. It's up to you."

This was impeccably fair and democratic, but there was just one problem—it made no sense. Sealing off the access points had been a coordinated action. If some intersections now opened up and other, rebel-camp intersections stayed occupied, delegates on their way out the meeting could just hang a right instead of a left, and they would be home free. Which, of course, is precisely what happened.

As I watched clusters of protesters get up and wander off while others stayed seated, defiantly guarding, well, nothing, it struck me as an apt metaphor for the strengths and weaknesses of this nascent activist network. There is no question that the communication culture that reigns on the Net is better at speed and volume than at synthesis. It is capable of getting tens of thousands of people to meet on the same street corner, placards in hand, but is far less adept at helping those same people to agree on what they are really asking for before they get to the barricades—or after they leave.

For this reason, an odd sort of anxiety has begun to set in after each demonstration: Was that it? When's the next one? Will it be as good, as big? To keep up the momentum, a culture of serial protesting is rapidly taking hold. My inbox is cluttered with entreaties to come to what promises to be "the next Seattle." There was Windsor and Detroit on June 4 for a "shutdown" of the Organization of American States, and Calgary a week later for the World Petroleum Congress; the Republican convention in Philadelphia in July and the Democratic convention in L.A. in August; the World Economic Forum's Asia Pacific Economic Summit on September 11 in Melbourne, followed shortly thereafter by anti-IMF demos on September 26 in Prague and then on to Quebec City for the Summit of the Americas in April 2001. Someone posted a message on the organizing e-mail list for the Washington demos: "Wherever they go, we shall be there! After this, see you in Prague!" But is this really what we want—a movement of meeting-stalkers, following the trade bureaucrats as if they were the Grateful Dead?

The prospect is dangerous for several reasons. Far too much expectation is being placed on these protests: The organizers of the D.C. demo, for instance, announced they would literally "shut down" two multi-billion dollar transnational institutions, at the same time as they attempted to convey sophisticated ideas about the fallacies of neoliberal economics to the stock-happy public. They simply couldn't do it; no single demo could, and it's only going to get harder. Seattle's direct-action tactics worked because they took the police by surprise. That won't happen again. Police have now subscribed to all the e-mail lists.

In an attempt to build a stable political structure to advance the movement between protests, Danaher has begun to fundraise for a "permanent Convergence Center" in Washington. The International Forum on Globalization, meanwhile, has been meeting since March in hopes of producing a 200-page policy paper by the end of the year. According to IFG director Jerry Mander, it won't be a manifesto but a set of principles and priorities, an early attempt, as he puts it, at "defining a new architecture" for the global economy.

Like the conference organizers at the Riverside Church, however, these initiatives will face an uphill battle. Most activists agree that the time has come to sit down and start discussing a positive agenda—but at whose table, and who gets to decide?

These questions came to a head at the end of May 2000 when Czech President Vaclav Havel offered to "mediate" talks between World Bank president James Wolfensohn and the protesters planning to disrupt the bank's September 26-28 meeting in Prague. There was no consensus among protest organizers about participating in the talks at Prague Castle, and, more to the point, there was no process in place to make the decision: no mechanism to select acceptable members of an activist delegation (some suggested an Internet vote) and no agreed-upon set of goals by which to measure the benefits and pitfalls of taking part. If Havel had reached out to the groups specifically dealing with debt and structural adjustment, like Jubilee 2000 or 50 Years Is Enough, the proposal would have been dealt with in a straightforward manner. But because he approached the entire movement as if it were a single unit, he sent those organizing the demonstrations into weeks of internal strife that remained unresolved.

Part of the problem is structural. Among most anarchists, who are doing a great deal of the grassroots organizing (and who got on-line way before the more established left), direct democracy, transparency, and community self-determination are not lofty political goals, they are fundamental tenets governing their own organizations. Yet many of the key NGOs, though they may share the anarchists' ideas about democracy in theory, are themselves organized as traditional hierarchies. They are run by charismatic leaders and executive boards, while their members send them money and cheer from the sidelines.

So how do you extract coherence from a movement filled with anarchists, whose greatest tactical strength so far has been its similarity to a swarm of mosquitoes? Maybe, as with the Internet itself, you don't do it by imposing a preset structure but rather by skillfully surfing the structures that are already in place. Perhaps what is needed is not a single political party but better links among the affinity groups; perhaps rather than moving toward more centralization, what is needed is further radical decentralization.

When critics say that the protesters lack vision, what they are really saying is that they lack an overarching revolutionary philosophy—like Marxism, democratic socialism, deep ecology, or social anarchy—on which they all agree. That is absolutely true, and for this we should be extraordinarily thankful.

At the moment, the anticorporate street activists are ringed by would-be leaders, anxious for the opportunity to enlist them as foot soldiers for their particular cause. At one end there is Michael Lerner and his conference at the Riverside Church, waiting to welcome all that inchoate energy in Seattle and Washington inside the framework of his "Politics of Meaning." At the other, there is John Zerzan in Eugene, Oregon, who isn't interested in Lerner's call for "healing" but sees the rioting and property destruction as the first step toward the collapse of industrialization and a return to "anarcho-primitivism": a pre-agrarian hunter-gatherer utopia. In between there are dozens of other visionaries, from the disciples of Murray Bookchin and his theory of social ecology, to certain sectarian Marxists who are convinced the revolution starts tomorrow, to devotees of Kalle Lasn, editor of Adbusters, and his watered-down version of revolution through "culture-jamming." And then there is the unimaginative pragmatism coming from some union leaders who, before Seattle, were ready to tack social clauses onto existing trade agreements and call it a day.

It is to this young movement's credit that it has as yet fended off all of these agendas and has rejected everyone's generously donated manifesto, holding out for an acceptably democratic, representative process to take its resistance to the next stage. Perhaps its true challenge is not finding a vision but rather resisting the urge to settle on one too quickly. If it succeeds in warding off the teams of visionaries-in-waiting, there will be some short-term public relations problems. Serial protesting will burn some people out. Street intersections will declare autonomy. And yes, young activists will offer themselves up like lambs—dressed, frequently enough, in actual lamb costumes—to *The New York Times* Op-Ed page for ridicule.

But so what? Already, this decentralized, multiheaded swarm of a movement has succeeded in educating and radicalizing a generation of activists around the world. Before it signs on to anyone's ten-point plan, it deserves the chance to see if, out of its chaotic network of hubs and spokes, something new, something entirely its own, can emerge.

Reprinted with permission from *The Nation*, July 10, 2000.

> *Labor is prior to, and independent of, capital. Capital is only the fruit of labor, and could never have existed if labor had not first existed. Labor is the superior of capital, and deserves much the higher consideration.*
>
> President Abraham Lincoln
> December 3, 1861

21

Baby Steps to a Global Revolution?
An Interview with Juliette Beck

Tamara Straus

The protests against transnational corporate power have begun to sink in. A year ago, a mass movement that raised such issues as corporate accountability and Third World debt seemed an impossibility. But since the shutdown of the World Trade Organization meetings in November 1999 and the protests against international lending institutions in Washington, D.C., it has become obvious that Americans—particularly young Americans—are not as apolitical as people have tended to think. A movement of young activists is afoot. And their target is not one politician or businessman, but an entire system of international capital that they insist is creating an intolerable corporate culture, strangling democratic freedoms, and further impoverishing countries of the Third World.

Juliette Beck, 27, is economic rights coordinator for Global Exchange, an international human rights group based in San Francisco. Since helping to organize the Seattle demonstrations and the World Bank-IMF protests, she has become one of the more visible leaders of the movement, profiled in *The New Yorker*, named among the "New Radicals" in *Time* magazine, and invited to speak on public TV and radio.

Q: If anticorporate globalism is becoming the political movement of our time, why is that so? What passions have corporate culture and Third World labor issues activated in young Americans?

Beck: I think what corporate America has imposed on people is a disconnection from reality, from the environment, from production processes. So when young people start connecting these issues, it also connects them to the people who are making their clothes, to the people who are picking their food. We realize that the corporations have created a very unjust and inhumane system, which brings people into action, quite literally. People realize that their clothes are made by girls in sweatshops who didn't have the opportunity to go to school as we do, and they know that's just morally wrong. They want to do something about it.

Q: Do you think the battle against globalization includes a police state mentality in the United States?

Beck: Absolutely. The only way these free trade agreements have been able to be perpetuated and the only way to prevent citizen uprisings against globalization is through military force. Here in the United States, as some people have begun to challenge the system of corporate globalization, we are experiencing an attack on our First Amendment rights. And it's going to be our challenge to make people aware of the connection between issues of justice and human rights abuses.

The fight against police brutality and the fight against the World Trade Organization are linked. They go hand in hand because we're all going to be subject to the same police state as we fight corporate globalism. Some of our friends from the global south, from the Philippines and El Salvador, watched the maneuvering of the police and their tactics in D.C. and they said, "Well, this is really familiar. Now we can see who trains our police."

In contrast to the undemocratic style of the police, one of the notable parts of the new activism is its organizational style, particularly activists' preference for consensual decision-making.

Q: Where does this nonhierarchical organizational style come from?

Beck: It's a very conscious decision by people who have been involved in activism for a long time in the antinuclear, environmental, and other movements. They know it strengthens us and is an alternative to traditional top-down, hierarchical decision making, which of course is what we're fighting against. I was enlightened to the consensus process by a group in Berkeley called the Art and Revolution Collective. Through them, I realized the power and utility of the consensus process in empowering every person in a group to be an organizer. Previously, what I found in my organizing was that when I had to go sleep or leave work everything stopped. Or when I got sick the campaign stopped because it was so much focused on one person. Well, with the consensus process, everyone is committed, everyone is engaged, and work can continue long past that one person. The action is self-perpetuating through this model. It's already achieved great success in that the mass actions we've organized in Seattle and Washington, D.C. have been decentralized and yet strategically connected. We subverted the WTO Seattle meeting this way.

Q: Are many of the new activists the progeny of former 1960s radicals and activists? Are we seeing a generational changing of the guard?

Beck: I come from a totally apolitical family. The people in my family are very opinionated but we didn't talk much about politics around the dinner table. It wasn't until I got to U.C. Berkeley that I started to be concerned about global issues. I think that people experience epiphanies in many different ways. Some find out about corporate subterfuge through their parents, some through friendships; others got turned on to environmental issues in college: They learn about recycling in college and get on the path there.

Q: What about the fact that most activists and protesters are middle class and white as well as in college, where they are benefiting directly from the wealth of corporations? How do young activists view this contradiction?

Beck: One of the main groups that has emerged in recent years is the Student Alliance to Reform Corporations (STARC), which started at Yale University and now has a couple hundred chapters across the United States. STARC was initially founded to get their colleges to pull out of irresponsible investments, to put a social and environmental screen on endowments and other funds. So I think that students are getting really sophisticated in understanding that their institutions are part of the problem and that they are an easy target. The reason students got involved in sweatshop issues is because they've been able to go back to their campuses and challenge their administrations around the issue of codes of conduct, questioning, for example, where the clothes that their university bookstore sells are coming from.

Q: Many women are serving as visible leaders in the mobilization for global justice. In addition to you, Hillary McQuie of the Direct Action Network and Njoki Njoroge Njehu of 50 Years Is Enough have received media attention. Yet many report that the movement is male-dominated. Is gender an important issue?

Beck: I think people involved in this movement are very sensitive to gender issues, and power relationships in general. The good facilitators always say: "Who hasn't spoken yet? Who hasn't voiced their opinion yet?" I think that as far as women getting the spotlight and being conscious of it, it's different. I see myself as doing work I'm committed to doing and I'm glad that I'm a woman and have an opportunity to inspire people. It's not a male-dominated movement. I think it's been a breath of fresh air that there are these women in the movement. We're really getting away from the idea that there are leaders at all here.

Q: What do you offer as an alternative to the system?
Beck: We believe in unleashing the people's creativity; that's

why we have so much emphasis on art. I think puppets are getting as much play as anything else. It's important to connect up creative art with creative politics, embrace the spirit of global music, techno, cutting-edge visual art. What we need is a whole new democratic culture.

Because the Direct Action Network is organizing around anarchist practices and principles, it's easy for some of the media to brand us as fringe. So we're having, frankly, problems with terminology in the movement right now. The mainstream media have also erroneously labeled us as flat-earthers and protectionists. They say we want to take people back to the Dark Ages and that we're opposed to globalization. On the contrary, we are for globalization—but a form of globalization that is grassroots and nonexploitative. In terms of protection, we're fighting to protect water and the land and natural resources that are being destroyed by corporations. Our interest is to protect human rights and workers' rights from corporate greed. The way the terms anarchism and protectionism are being used is clouding the real issues.

Q: Is there an effort to link American activists with international organizations waging similar campaigns against corporate power?

Beck: People around the world have been fighting against the World Bank and the IMF for decades. Thousands of people have taken to the streets against IMF policies in Latin America, Africa, Asia, and the Middle East. So the fact that we had thousands of people taking to the streets to protest the World Bank and the IMF in the United States is nothing new in a global context, it's just the first time it happened here. Frankly, we're playing catch-up to the rest of the world. As far as linking organizations, the movement is incredibly decentralized. Yet we can remain decentralized and be strong because of the Internet. A lot of the solidarity work that's being done right now is around Chiapas and supporting the Zapatistas. The rebellion that started on the day NAFTA went into effect [January 1, 1994] became known because the shot was heard around the Web. Because the Zapatistas communicate through the Internet, people are instantly connected to them.

The question is: If what we're experiencing are the baby steps of a global revolution against corporate greed and unmitigated corporate power, can it be peaceful? I'm for nonviolence training and a peaceful movement here in the United States. I am working for a movement of protesters who can confront corporate power in a meaningful, deliberate way without taking up arms.

Q: Can a large group of people really be mobilized to protest corporate power?

Beck: Well, it's actually quite easy to do that because the corporations are so dependent on image and brand name. All you have to do is take the swoosh and put a cross through it and people know what that means in regard to Nike's sweatshop practices. We launched an advertising campaign against The Gap. They have an ad slogan that says "Everybody in Leather," "Everybody in Khakis," etc. So our campaign said, "Everybody in Sweatshops" with a picture of a garment worker underneath. I think we can use corporations' advertising and brand name to turn their tactics on their head and show the darker side of corporate activities. Because they spend so much money on advertising and their image, it makes them very vulnerable.

At Global Exchange, we've been building a campaign around fair trade coffee to get students and their universities to only buy coffee grown and harvested under fair trade conditions. It's taken off like gangbusters. We've had a huge victory with Starbucks. Before we even kicked off our campaign, Starbucks agreed to the demands of carrying fair trade coffee in their stores. It's a victory for small coffee farmers; it's going to triple their income.

Q: Are you surprised by the new activism? For twenty years progressives have sat in their armchairs, occasionally giving donations or signing petitions, but now a lot of young people are getting out there to march and protest. Why do you think this is happening?

Beck: We're evolving so quickly. I did not expect this to come out of Seattle. One of the things I've always said is that activism is not an extracurricular activity. It's a way of life. You have to be a vigilant and active participant in democracy or we get what we've got now: a hypocrisy of democracy. The whole system is out of whack and unbalanced. Corporations are in the driver's seat, writing the rules of the world economy, which will impact everyone on earth. So we need to democratize economic decision making, so that it's not just free-market economists and corporate executives who are making the policies that effect everyone on the planet.

Q: Marc Cooper recently wrote in the *LA Weekly* that it's not clear that A16 strengthened the fledgling alliance between labor and the blue-green coalition that emerged after Seattle. How do you plan to keep the alliances that were formed out of Seattle and Washington together?

Beck: We have to pick the issues that unite us. There will definitely be a fair trade coalition following up on our work in Seattle and D.C. The movement is launching a campaign to "shrink or sink the World Trade Organization." Right now it's just been a process of getting to know one another, building trust, and when that happens, anything is possible in terms of connecting people and building a huge movement.

Bankers' Salaries Go Through the Roof

IMF Managing Director Horst Koehler of Germany, receives an annual tax-free salary of $308,460. That's equivalent to more than $500,000 in taxable income. Koehler's counterpart at the World Bank, James Wolfensohn, nets $248,000 per year.

22

Defunding the Fund, Running on the Bank

Patrick Bond

Two ordinarily impenetrable financial institutions—the IMF and World Bank—have finally come into focus for activists, in a way that sharpens the discussion surrounding globalization and popular resistance. Around thirty thousand protesters joined the Mobilization for Global Justice in Washington, D.C., on April 16, 2000, capping a week that began ominously. It started with a chilly and poorly attended Jubilee 2000 USA debt-relief rally on April 9 (controversially addressed by neoliberal Clinton economist Gene Sperling); a protectionist and vaguely xenophobic "No Blank Check for China" demonstration at the Capitol on April 12, which included 15,000 workers organized by the AFL-CIO; and dozens of other related events. Auspiciously, in contrast, the bulk of the A16/17 protesters rallied around a call for the Fund and Bank to be defunded (not reformed), just as most Seattle demonstrators had surpassed reformist leadership in relation to the World Trade Organization (WTO). God smiled on the 16th, giving the Mobilization the warmth and sunshine denied the Jubilee reformers, and many left Washington convinced that a campaign to attack the funding of the IMF and World Bank is a sensible next step.

Socialists across the world should be heartened. With momentum captured by the Mobilization, rather than by the reformist Jubilee, enormous ideological progress and political maturity can be claimed and consolidated. A16/17 was built upon a militant, internationalist platform and slogan—"Break the Bank, Defund the Fund, Dump the Debt!"—endorsed by a coalition of forces as strong and diverse as Seattle's.

The legal rally/march was joined by initially nervous trade unionists, NGO developmentalists, and environmentalists. Skillfully, the Mobilization's official core of left-leaning Washington think tank and NGO staff—notably, 50 Years is Enough, Alliance for Global Justice, Center for Economic and Policy Research, Center for Economic Justice, the Nader group Essential Action, and Jobs with Justice—helped to merge (at least temporarily) the very different agendas of inside-the-Beltway bureaucrats and grassroots activists. Labor/NGO/green officials have historically wobbled when faced with global political-economy issues, as a result of the disadvantageous balance of forces prior to Seattle, their often-debilitating ties to the Democratic Party, and a *faux* professionalism heightened by dependence upon bourgeois funders. The AFL-CIO even supported the $18 billion recapitalization of the IMF in late 1998, after some deal-making with the Clinton administration.

The activists, in contrast, were anxious to conduct a joyous symphony of Seattle-like lockdowns and street parties to blockade the Bank/Fund spring meetings. To do so, they introduced a cultural liberation ambience virtually unknown to Washington, utilizing radical participatory democracy and affinity-group cell structures in strategy sessions and trainings facilitated by striking young talents from the Direct Action Network (DAN).

Results included abundant forms of civil disobedience and 1,300 arrests. Unlike Seattle, the Revolutionary Anti-Capitalist Bloc of black-clad anarchists worked in harmony with those carrying out nonviolent civil disobedience and had the honor of attracting a police helicopter devoted solely to trailing their movements across Washington on A16.

Most importantly for our purposes here, the Mobilization drew the economic, social, and environmental concerns of the global

South far deeper into the fabric of the U.S. movement than ever before. Granted, the protest failed to prevent the Fund/Bank meetings, due to the massive police presence. No matter, the combination of thorough preparation and the large size of the turnout in Washington helped raise public consciousness about the Fund and Bank to unprecedented levels; brought sympathetic activists from different constituencies into successful coalition; taught organizers a great deal about Washington logistics (and how they can really be gummed up next time); showed South allies the extent of solidarity possibilities, encouraging them to intensify their own local critiques of the Fund/Bank; and facilitated a long-overdue split among development-NGOs (a group of twenty-two conservative organizations under the banner of "Interaction" sent a self-discrediting endorsement note to the Bank and Fund).

These protests have set an excellent stage for several years of intense grassroots campaigning across the globe aimed at closing the Bretton Woods twins, thus fundamentally reorienting our understanding of development finance and, in the process, restructuring power relations in ways that could benefit radical political movements across the South. Of course, an activist focus on the institutional forms of global capitalist mismanagement—namely the Bank, the IMF, and WTO—might detract from an understanding of both the capital accumulation process and class-based resistance, and hence lead to partial and imperfect strategic insights about power and social transformation. In addition, a focus on these global institutions might lead us to neglect national and regional issues and areas in which resistance might be more fruitful. "Bond-boycotting" the Bank and defunding the Fund should be supported as integral and unifying components of a broader mobilization for class, gender, ethnic, and environmental justice.

The IMF, the World Bank, and Imperialism

In 1944, the Bretton Woods resort in New Hampshire hosted a conference chaired by Harry Dexter White, representing the

U.S. Treasury, and John Maynard Keynes, representing Britain (but more broadly, the interests of the vast majority of countries then in debt). The overarching problem was, simply, the restoration of global capitalist order at a time when capitalists were profoundly discredited (partly thanks to associations with Nazism) or were otherwise in political-economic retreat, and when socialism appeared to be a dangerous specter, not only because of the U.S.S.R.'s durability but because communist and labor movements were resurgent in Europe. Reflecting the power of U.S. capital, White was able to establish the dollar as the world's primary currency and to construct the Fund and Bank so they could be controlled from the White House and U.S. Treasury.

Although the Fund initially encouraged nation-state exchange controls so as to limit capital flight, the two institutions founded at Bretton Woods would soon reverse that formula by promoting the globalization of capital over the globalization of people. The Fund was meant to balance the accounts of payments between countries (through money exchanged in trade and financial transactions), while the World Bank would make injections of project finance, starting in war-ravaged Western Europe and later in the global south. A few years later, the WTO's seeds were sown in the founding conference of the General Agreement on Tariffs and Trade (GATT) in Havana.

It was only in the late 1970s that the full significance of the IMF, World Bank, and GATT became evident; they were institutions that could solidify the control of capital in the North over that in the South during a period of capitalist crisis marked by a financial explosion, stagnating wages, intensifying environmental degradation, and declining living standards in the global south. They proved very useful in shifting the costs of various recent international financial crises from the rich capitalist nations onto those less powerful. And they contributed to the collapse of several decades' worth of ordinary people's living standards across the South since the late 1970s, in Eastern Europe since the late 1980s, and in emerging markets since the mid 1990s.

During this period, the Fund and Bank acquired a qualitatively new role: coordination power over both economic policymaking and financial/aid flows in subordinate countries (though still through the overall permission of the U.S. Treasury Department and consistent with the State Department's agenda). Fund and Bank coordination has meant not merely the certification of countries' policymakers as sufficiently pro-market (i.e., especially welcoming of currency devaluation, state shrinkage, loss of national economic sovereignty and inflowing financial, trade, and foreign direct investments, partly to capture privatized assets at healthy discounts and partly just to speculate).

From the early 1980s, the Fund and Bank also played a crucial debt-policing role, firming up the weakened balance sheets of those Northern commercial banks and investment funds that were exposed due to the demise of unpopular client-dictators during the 1980s, and late 1990s speculative fiascoes in "emerging market" countries. Fund/Bank bailouts were arranged so that New York, London, Frankfurt, Zurich, and Tokyo banks could recover (and indeed prosper) from 1980s-era Third World debt (which remained on the liability side of borrowers' balance sheets), as well as from the devastation of currencies associated with speculative runs on Mexico (early 1995), South Africa (early 1996 and mid-1998), Southeast Asia (1997-98), South Korea (early 1998), Russia (periodic but especially mid-1998), and Brazil and Ecuador (early 1999).

The negative impact of World Bank and IMF policies was so stark and obvious that professional and intellectual justification was required. The protectionist and inward-oriented economic policies of many developing nations were attacked by proponents of a laissez-faire, "neoliberal" philosophy consistent with the liberalizing interests of international financial/commercial capitals. The "Washington Consensus,"—a market-fundamentalist worldview imposed by the United States through the IMF and the World Bank and supported by associated think tanks—insisted that the alleged merits (future growth and prosperity) of free-market "structural adjustment" outweighed the enormous short-term economic, social, gender, generational, public health, and environmental costs.

There have been moments of mass popular resistance to the IMF and the World Bank, but these have rarely been coordinated to challenge state power and neoliberalism more generally. At times, third-world nationalism has sounded resurgent, as in Venezuela under Chavez, but up to now resistance in this tradition has quickly fizzled out once Fund/Bank screws were tightened, or worse, has turned inward to repress the left, as in Mahathir's Malaysia and Mugabe's Zimbabwe. More hopeful signs include the emergence of Zapatismo in 1994; Korean workers' battles against IMF restructuring; periodic mobilizations by the Brazilian Movement of the Landless (MST); the graduation of India's National Alliance of People's Movements from world-class protests against dams and genetic engineering to campaigns against neoliberalism more generally; the January 2000 uprising of Ecuadoran Indians against neoliberalism; the emergence of Thailand's Forum of the Poor at a major U.N. meeting in Bangkok in February 2000; the dramatic April revolt of Bolivians against water privatization; and protests in Chiang Mai, Thailand, against the Asian Development Bank meetings in May. Though none generated conclusive victories, they provide important, if incomplete, lessons for other protest trajectories, alongside recent North-led campaigns to halt the Multilateral Agreement on Investment (MAI), ban landmines, halt toxic-waste dumping, and prevent the WTO from launching its Seattle round.

The IMF and World Bank are central to imperialism's reproduction, both in terms of their power to dictate how the poor countries will "develop" and their power to displace the effects of capitalist crisis onto the world's poor. They carry out their mandate in a way that entails both universal suffering by subordinate classes and damage to the environment. But in the wake of the April 2000 protests in Washington and the September protests in Prague, there are prospects for a more sustainable and radical resistance strategy. For even if the Fund/Bank represent merely institutional vehicles, they are exceptionally important targets, at least until more serious challenges are generated by shop-floor, community, feminist, and environmentalist protest to local and global manifestations of the mode of production itself. Indeed, campaigning to abolish the Bretton Woods institutions and the interests they serve offers possibly the best focus for global class struggle in all its various spheres that the left has yet witnessed.

Strategic Divergences

There are those, however, who suggest that abolishing the IMF and the World Bank is an inappropriate radical strategy. Some envision the development of a world state. Such a state— the logical consequence of the rapid globalization of capital— would imply the creation of a global working class (and its party). Such a global working class could then contend directly with capital, struggling for environmental protection, wealth redistribution, peacekeeping, and human rights policing. Socialist intellectuals working from the world-systems tradition, social justice philosophy, and "cosmopolitan democracy" theory are advancing such a case.

Here are Terry Boswell and Christopher Chase-Dunn in *The Spiral of Capitalism and Socialism*: "The interstate system is the political structure that stands behind the maneuverability of capital and its ability to escape organized workers and other social constraints on profitable accumulation. While a world state may at first be largely controlled by capitalists, the very existence of such a state will provide a single focus for struggles to socially regulate investment decisions and to create a more balanced, egalitarian, and ecologically sound form of production and distribution."[1]

Skeptical, University of Chicago philosopher Iris Young recommends closure of the IMF and Bank, which "do not even pretend to be inclusive and democratic." Instead, she argues that a "reasonable goal" is reform of the United Nations, "the best existing starting point for building global democratic institutions... As members of the General Assembly, nearly all the world's peoples today are represented at the U.N." Moreover, the U.N. is a site where imperial powers "seek legitimacy for some of their international actions" and where states "at least appear to be cooperative and interested in justice." Likewise, civil society organizations have mobilized around U.N. events and issues.[2]

The primary problem here is that given the existing and foreseeable balance of international power, hopes for eco-social progress through world state-building are utopian, maybe dangerously so. Far more likely, if this course is pursued, is an expansion of neoliberalism, the universal rule of property, and the commodification of all aspects of daily life everywhere, with consequent destruction of noncapitalist ecological, social, and economic processes, amplified through far more devastating punishment by the "international community" for transgression by oppositional states or popular movements.

Still other socialists insist upon a global regulatory agenda to reign in the power of capital, including the adoption of export sanctions (usually through trade law) against countries where child labor, health and safety, rights to trade-union organizing, and comparable social and environmental problems emerge. This debate is beyond the scope of my Fund/Bank argument, but at least one point should be firmly stated here. The first principle of political solidarity entails not promoting the power of an oppressor nation against an oppressed nation, especially without the consent and indeed request of the people most affected. Exceptions include Northern boycotts against goods from (or finance to) apartheid-era South Africa and Burma, where sanctions called for by mass/popular democratic movements translated into a strategic attack on local oppressors. In cases where sanctions do not explicitly link to a mass movement's own liberation, it is strategically absurd to lend legitimacy to international institutions like the WTO, World Bank, and IMF (as well as powerful Northern governments) for imposition of new controls on what is already a terribly unequal trade, investment, and financing relationship with the South.

A parallel problem emerged in campaigning against the Fund and Bank during the reformism of the early 1980s that strengthened, not weakened, the two institutions. Indeed, some in Jubilee 2000 North chapters (the United States, United Kingdom, Germany, and Japan) have viewed the current upsurge in protest as an opportunity to lobby for a greater, not lesser role, for the Fund, Bank, and their discredited "Highly Indebted Poor Countries" debt-relief initiative. An impressive Jubilee South initiative emerged from debtor countries in 1999, yet it spends an unfortunately excessive amount of energy and time arguing against the highly conditional, half-hearted reforms that Jubilee Northerners seek, allied with the Pope, Jeffrey Sachs (director of the Harvard Institute for International Development and the mind behind the devastating economic "shock therapy" in Russia in the early 1990s), and bourgeois politicians.

In five areas—environmental protection, gender awareness, transparency, community participation, and post-Washington Consensus economics—reformers can claim limited victories. But those very wins have provided the Bank and Fund a coat of whitewash, barely disguising their complete dedication to hardcore neoliberalism with talk of sustainability—in the process dividing unsophisticated opponents. Empowered by the Bank's plagiarism of NGO rhetoric, some inside-the-Beltway policy wonks (e.g., in the often admirable international advocacy office of Friends of the Earth) are even suggesting a dramatic switch in Bank lending towards sectors like basic education—"Public funds for public good."

How far can such reforms go? The long, ugly history of these organizations suggests not very far. It is now widely acknowledged, for example, that maverick Bank chief economist Joe Stiglitz was fired so that James Wolfensohn could win another term as Bank president from his boss, U.S. Treasury Secretary

Lawrence Summers, who harbors a longstanding grudge against Stiglitz. Because the central players within the IMF and Bank clearly remain committed to Washington Consensus orthodoxy, and reforms won to date have been profoundly unsatisfying, organizers in the Mobilization for Global Justice could seek and achieve a rare clarity of radical strategic purpose—to defund the institutions or at least limit their power.

Consider the words of radical third-world guru of international economics, Walden Bello, director of Focus on the Global South in Bangkok, explaining his shift to a pro-abolition position: "Seventy per cent of the Bank's non-aid lending is concentrated in 11 countries, while the Bank's 145 other member countries are left to divide the remaining 30 percent. Moreover, 80 percent of World Bank resources have gone, not to poor countries with poor credit ratings and investment ratings, but to countries that could have raised the money in international private capital markets owing to their having investment grade or high yield ratings. In terms of achieving a positive development impact, the Bank's own evaluation of its projects shows an outstanding 55-60 percent failure rate. The failure rate is particularly high in the poorest countries, where it ranges from 65-70 percent. And these are the very countries that are supposed to be the main targets of the Bank's antipoverty approach... Rather than expect the highly paid World Bank technocrats who live in the affluent suburbs of Northern Virginia to do the impossible—designing anti-poverty programs for folks from another planet (poor people in the Sahel)—it would be more effective to abolish an institution that has made a big business out of "ending poverty," and completely devolve the work to local, national, and regional institutions better equipped to attack the causes of poverty."[3]

After the IMF and World Bank Are Abolished

Karl Marx once asserted that prior to constructing world socialism, each working class must first deal with its own national bourgeoisie, a position that incorporated a fairly advanced critique of early colonial globalization. Global deconstruction and national reconstruction may be a useful formula with which to begin to conclude. Implicit in the argument sketched out above is that the nation-state requires space out from under the boot of global financial capitalism, especially the spiked heel represented by Fund/Bank missions that so decisively squeeze and shift power relations at the domestic level.

And there are no shortage of national-scale class and political struggles. During the late 1990s, mass strikes by national workers' movements shook Nigeria, Indonesia, Paraguay, Taiwan (1994); Bolivia, Canada, France (1995); Argentina, Brazil, Canada, Greece, Italy, South Korea, Spain, Venezuela (1996); Belgium, Colombia, Ecuador, Haiti, South Korea (1997); and many other important sites of East Asian, East European, African, and Latin American proletarian suffering when the neoliberal economic crisis intensified in 1998-1999.

Yet a political warning is clearly in order, this time from David Harvey: "Withdrawing to the nation-state as the exclusive strategic site of class organization and struggle is to court failure (as well as to flirt with nationalism and all that entails). This does not mean the nation-state has become irrelevant—indeed it has become more relevant than ever. But the choice of spatial scale is not 'either/or' but 'both/and' even though the latter entails confronting serious contradictions."[4]

If local, national, and regional development finance is appropriate, then the technical (not political, moral, environmental) reasons to have a Fund and Bank evaporate. Such was the viewpoint of the African National Congress (ANC) in its 1994 Reconstruction and Development Programme (RDP), in a sentence won only after much left-wing lobbying—"The RDP must use foreign debt financing only for those elements of the program that can potentially increase our capacity for earning foreign exchange" (The ANC broke more than one such promise, but it is the principle here that is worth careful reflection.).

The motivation for avoiding hard-currency loans for "development" was the ANC left's fear of the rising cost of repayment on foreign debt, once the currency declines, and the use of hard currency to pay *not* for initiating a basic education project but instead for repaying illegitimate apartheid debt; importing luxury goods for the rich; and replacing local workers with inappropriate, job-killing, dependency-inducing technology from abroad. In sum, why take a U.S. dollar loan for building and staffing a small rural school that has virtually no foreign input costs?

If real development comes from local resources (only a tiny fraction of basic-need inputs in most developing countries require foreign loans), and if the hard currency needed to import petroleum or other vital inputs can usually be readily supplied by export credit agencies (competing against each other, in contrast to centralized financial power and coordination in Washington), the basic rationale for the World Bank falls away. And instead of relying upon the IMF to maintain a positive balance of payments when fickle international financial inflows dry up or run away frightened, third world countries that in the future climb out from under the heel of the Fund and Bank could realistically impose Malaysian-style exchange controls and tax unnecessary imports. They would also have more freedom to default on illegitimate debt.

In short, the South ultimately shouldn't need a dollar-denominated Fund and Bank for development. Indeed, it is probable that only when Washington's institutional power fades that local, national, and perhaps regional development finance officials can reacquire the ability they once enjoyed, a few decades ago, to tame their own financial markets. (This entailed state interest-rate subsidies, directed credit, prescribed asset requirements on institutional investors, community reinvestment mandates, and other means of socializing financial capital.)

Can We Do It?

The one remaining point to make is the easiest, most practical answer in this article—is defunding actually feasible? The same question was asked of those advocating antiapartheid financial sanctions, and answered in the affirmative in 1985, just a few years after campaigning became serious. In addition to defunding the Fund through popular pressure on the U.S. Congress—and indeed all parliaments—to deny further resources, activists returning from A16 began taking advantage of the Bank's extreme reliance upon international bond markets. Nearly 80 percent of Bank funds for lending comes from bonds, making them the most compelling pressure point and local handle for the medium-term struggle. To this end, a "World Bank Bond Boycott"—initiated by Haitian, South African, Brazilian, and many other activists and debt campaigners across the world—was launched on April 10 with help from two U.S. groups, the Center for Economic Justice and Global Exchange. Berkeley City Council offered the initial commitment that its municipal fund managers won't buy World Bank bonds. Oakland and San Francisco soon followed. All investors of conscience—pension funds, churches, university endowments, individuals—are being asked not to profit from poverty and ecological destruction fostered by the World Bank. A frightened *Washington Post* lead editorial on April 11 called the Bond Boycott "crazy." In coming months, activists will prove establishment concerns entirely justified, as they did with the financial sanctions that helped sink the Botha and de Klerk regimes in Pretoria.

The attraction of defunding the Washington institutions, as campaign themes that U.S. and other Northern activists can easily invoke as part of a general consciousness-raising exercise about the Fund and Bank, is that it correlates to South campaigns that also aim to weaken, expel, and shut down the Bretton Woods twins. The basis for the growing campaign in Johannesburg, for example, to kick the Bank out of South Africa, is that Bank staff have played crucial roles in policies ranging from macroeconomic structural adjustment to the privatization of Johannesburg's municipal services. The more the Fund and Bank are active in a given capital city, the faster local life gets reduced to mere commodity circulation. Evicting the Washington economists who work so closely with local collaborator elites is another step in changing the balance of forces in most domestic contexts. But it is also a warm-up for the broader, deeper campaign to decommodify and destratify South societies. And for radical economists in the South who link the particular actions and ideology of IMF and Bank missions to the way in which the broader global capitalist crisis of overaccumulation plays out, it is no accident that we can locate both power and vulnerability within the sphere of finance—as Karl Marx, Paul Sweezy, Harry Magdoff, Richard Grossman, and others have reminded us.

For socialist activists, therefore, defunding the IMF and breaking the Bank can raise consciousness, dramatically improve global and local power balances, generate new thinking about radical local financing alternatives that lead to development independent of imperialism, and contribute to an internationalist solidarity unfettered by controversy over reform of global financial institutions.

A16 gave thousands of activists an initial opportunity to run on the Bank and the IMF. The follow-up challenge is to keep those institutions running until they drop from exhaustion.

FOOTNOTES

1. Terry Boswell and Christopher Chase-Dunn, *The Spiral of Capitalism and Socialism* (Boulder, CO: Lynn Reiner, 1999).

2. Iris Marion Young, *Inclusion and Democracy* (Oxford: Oxford University Press, 2000), Chapter 7.

3. Walden Bello, "Meltzer Report on Bretton Woods Twins Builds Case for Abolition but Hesitates," *Focus on Trade* 48 (April 2000).

4. David Harvey, "The Geography of Class Power," in Leo Panitch and Colin Leys, eds., *The Communist Manifesto Now: Socialist Register 1998* (New York: Monthly Review Press, 1998), p. 72.

23

Structural Adjusment Is Hitting the U.S. Too

Anuradha Mittal

There is enough evidence on how policies of the World Bank, International Monetary Fund (IMF) and the World Trade Organization (WTO) have come to connote colonialism and a dominating world capitalist system for the Third World. The unregulated flow of global capital has placed the fate of developing economies at the mercy of Wall Street traders. However, nations of the South are not the only victims of this process. There is also a "South" in the North—right here in the United States—that is being harmed by domestic policies of the U.S. government, such as the "Contract With America" and "welfare reform." This is the same package of policies imposed by the World Bank and the IMF on developing countries.

With the rise of neoliberalism on a worldwide scale, Third World countries have faced rampant privatization and the removal of barriers to trade via structural adjustment programs imposed by the World Bank and the IMF. In the United States, supply-side economics, or "Reaganomics," have continued uninterrupted under the Bush and Clinton administrations. In England it was called "Thatcherism" but has continued virtually uninterrupted under the "New Labor" government. Regardless of where it has taken place, the onslaught has been remarkably similar: debts and government deficits accumulated through military overspending and tax cuts for the rich are being repaid on the backs of the poor, women, immigrants, people of color and workers.

In both rich and poor nations, dislocations from economic and corporate restructuring, and from dismantling the institutions of social protection, have resulted in greater insecurity in jobs and incomes. Never before has there been such a stark contrast between the mass of working families waging daily struggles for survival and pervasive media chatter about unprecedented prosperity.

The 'Third Worldization' of America

The double squeeze by corporate America and a U.S. government catering to corporate interest has forced Americans to give back quite a bit. For example:

• Despite glowing media reports on the booming economy, as estimated 46 million Americans, nearly 17 percent of the population, live below the official poverty line.

• The top 2.7 million people have as much income as the bottom 100 million. The richest one percent of Americans are projected to have as much income as the bottom 38 percent. Wealth is even more concentrated, with the wealthiest one percent of households owning nearly 40 percent of the nation's wealth. The bottom 80 percent own just 16 percent of the nation's wealth. Further widening this inequality, CEOs of U.S. corporations pocketed 419 times the average wage of a blue collar worker in 1998.

• According to the Report on Household Food Security put out by the U.S. Department of Agriculture in 1999, an estimated 36 million Americans in 10.5 million households do not have access to adequate food.

• Economic growth is not reducing hunger because, even though more households are in the workforce, their take-home pay is not enough to feed their families. A full-time worker at minimum wage earns $9,512 a year. For a family of four, that puts the family income well below the federal poverty line of $17,072.

• A survey of 26 cities released in December 1999 by the U.S. Conference of Mayors shows that hunger and homelessness has grown unabated, despite an expanding national economy. Among two key findings of the 1999 Status Report on Hunger and Homelessness in America's cities, demand for emergency food related assistance during 1999 grew at the highest level since 1992 (18 percent over the previous year), and demand for emergency housing related assistance grew at the highest level since 1994. Twenty-one percent of requests for emergency food assistance are estimated to have gone unmet.

• The government has responded to this crisis by passing legislation such as welfare reform which has resulted in 11 million families, including eight million with children, losing their income. This happened despite the fact that total federal spending for food programs *before* welfare reform was only 2.5 percent of the federal budget. More than half of the $54 billion in welfare cuts are coming from food stamps that 25 million poor Americans depended upon. Over 80 percent of food stamps go to families with children. These cuts have resulted in increased hunger.

• In 1997, Second Harvest, the country's largest chain of food banks provided food for almost 26 million people, nearly ten percent of America's population. Even then it had to turn away 2.3 million people. To compensate fully for the government cuts, each of the 350,000 churches in the United States would have to contribute an additional $150,000 and many churches do not have a budget this large. To make up for the shortfall, the non-profit sector would have to distribute a total of 24.5 billion pounds of food over the next six years, four times more then the current distribution and enough to fill five million Army National Guard Trucks.

• The number of Americans who lack health insurance continues to rise, climbing to 44.3 million in spite of a prosperous economy.

• Some seven to eight million Americans are homeless.

• In the Unites States approximately 20.7 percent of the population age 16 to 65 is functionally illiterate; the majority of them are low-paid workers such as farm workers, domestic workers and other who labor long hours in low-paying jobs.

Indeed, structural adjustment Washington-style is giving the U.S. a Third World appearance: rising poverty, widespread homelessness, greater inequality and social polarization. But perhaps it is the state of children that most starkly captures the 'Third Worldization' of America. Today, the United States has the highest rate of child poverty among the industrialized countries, with one in every five children growing up in poverty. The number of children living at or below one-half of the poverty line increased by 426,000 between 1996 and 1997. About 20 percent of all children under the age of 18, or 14 million, live in food insecure homes.

Impact of IMF/World Bank Policies on Americans

• The U.S. trade deficit has mushroomed from about $107 billion in 1990 to more than $270 billion in 1999. A study by the Institute for Policy Studies shows how World Bank/IMF policy lending has contributed to the increase of the U.S. trade deficit by prescribing currency devaluations in debtor countries, which make U.S. imports more expensive, and by prescribing cuts in government spending, which lead to job losses and reduced purchasing power of people to buy U.S. goods.

• Although U.S. unemployment is at a record low, the fact that U.S. imports are far outstripping exports has displaced U.S. jobs, particularly in the manufacturing sector. More than 530,000 U.S. manufacturing jobs were lost between March 1998 and September 1999. This is significant because manufacturing jobs generally pay better and more often offer fringe benefits such as health insurance and pension coverage than other sectors that employ non-college graduates.

• World Bank and IMF programs have also contributed to downward pressure on U.S. wages by prescribing the lifting of controls on investment and so-called "labor market flexibility" measures that weaken unions. These policies have contributed to the global mobility of corporations, increasing their power to bargain down wages and working conditions here in the United States. Although real wages in the United States rose slightly in 1998 and 1999, low-income workers, including large numbers of people of color and women, saw their wages erode during the 1990s. Even some globalization proponents admit that 20-25 percent of the increase in U.S. inequality may be due to import competition and employers moving (or threatening to move) to developing countries where they can take advantage of lax enforcement of worker rights.

Corporate-driven structural adjustment has triggered severe social stress in both the North and the South. The United States, after dismantling many of the social mechanisms of the New Deal, has addressed the discontent through punitive measures. U.S. expenditures on criminal justice have increased four times faster than the budget for education, and twice as fast as outlays on hospitals and health. Today the United States has achieved the dubious distinction of imprisoning a larger share of its population than any other nation.

To counter this wave of corporate driven structural adjustment, it is essential that we promote the common interests of the peoples of the South and the North. This entails forging, across borders, an alternative economic vision, one that brings the economy back under the control of the community, one that fosters solidarity instead of polarization.

> *Every person must decide whether to walk in the light of creative altruism or in the darkness of destructive selfishness. This is the judgment. Life's most persistent and urgent question is, "What are you doing for others?"*
> Rev. Martin Luther King, Jr.

24

Demands for Transforming the World Bank and the IMF

50 Years Is Enough Network

We call for the immediate suspension of the policies and practices that have caused widespread poverty and suffering among the world's peoples and damage to the world's environment. We assert the responsibility of the World Bank and the International Monetary Fund, together with the World Trade Organization, for an unjust world economic system.

We issue this call in the name of global justice, in solidarity with the peoples of the Global South struggling for survival and dignity in the face of unjust, imperialistic economic policies. Only when the coercive powers of the international financial institutions are rescinded shall governments be accountable first and foremost to the will of their people for equitable economic development.

Only when a system that allocates power chiefly to the wealthiest nations for the purpose of dictating the policies of the poorer ones is reversed shall nations and their people be able to forge bonds—economic and otherwise—based on mutual respect and the common needs of the planet and its inhabitants. Only when the well-being of all, including the most vulnerable people and ecosystems, is given priority over corporate profits shall we achieve genuine sustainable development and create a world of justice, equality, and peace.

With these ends in mind, we make the following demands of the World Bank and the International Monetary Fund:

1. That the IMF and World Bank cancel all debts owed them. Any funds required for this purpose should come from positive net capital and assets held by those institutions.

2. That the IMF and World Bank immediately cease imposing the economic austerity measures known as structural adjustment and/or other macroeconomic "reforms," which have exacerbated poverty and inequality, as conditions of loans, credits, or debt relief. This requires both the suspension of those conditions in existing programs and an abandonment of any version of the Heavily Indebted Poor Countries (HIPC) initiative which is founded on the concept of debt relief in exchange for policy reform.

3. That the IMF and World Bank accept responsibility for the disastrous impact of structural adjustment policies by paying reparations to the peoples and communities who have borne that impact. These funds should come from the institutions' positive net capital and assets, and should be distributed through democratically controlled mechanisms.

4. That the World Bank Group pay reparations to peoples relocated and otherwise harmed by its large projects (such as dams) and compensate governments for repayments made on projects which World Bank evaluations judge to be economic failures. A further evaluation should determine which World Bank projects have failed on social, cultural, and environmental grounds, and appropriate compensation should be paid. The funds for these payments should come from the institution's positive net capital and assets, and should be distributed through democratically-determined mechanisms.

5. That the World Bank Group immediately cease providing advice and resources through its division devoted to private-sector investments to advance the goals associated with corporate globalization, such as privatization and liberalization, and that

private-sector investments currently held be liquidated to provide funds for the reparations demanded above.

6. That the agencies and individuals within the World Bank Group and IMF who are complicit in abetting corruption, as well as their accomplices in borrowing countries, be prosecuted, and that those responsible, including the institutions involved, provide compensation for resources stolen and damage done.

7. That the future existence, structure, and policies of international institutions such as the World Bank Group and the IMF be determined through a democratic, participatory, and transparent process. The process must accord full consideration of the interests of the peoples most affected by the policies and practices of the institutions, and include a significant role for all parts of civil society.

Because these demands would effectively mean the end of the World Bank and the IMF in their current form, we harbor no illusion that the institutions' directors will accept them immediately. It is very possible, then, that the elimination of these institutions will be required for the realization of global economic and political justice.

We commit to work toward the defunding of the IMF and World Bank by opposing further government allocations to them (in the form of either direct contributions or the designation of callable capital) and supporting campaigns such as boycotting World Bank bonds and calling for reparations until these demands have been met.

We need to break the power of the World Bank over developing countries, just as the divestment movement helped break the power of the Apartheid regime in South Africa; this is why we support the boycott of World Bank bonds.

Dennis Brutus
Jubilee 2000 South Africa

25

Boycotting World Bank Bonds

Neil Watkins and Kevin Danaher

The World Bank Bond Boycott unites grassroots organizations from more than ten countries in an effort to pressure the World Bank by attacking the major source of its funding: the selling of bonds in commercial bond markets.

If we can convince institutional investors (e.g., universities, churches, trade unions, city and state governments) to publicly announce that they will not buy World Bank bonds, we can attack the AAA ("triple A") rating of World Bank bonds. By making the bonds less desirable to investors, we can weaken the Bank and pressure it for change.

Do you remember the impact the divestment movement had on South Africa's white minority rulers by cutting them off from their foreign sources of capital? The divestment struggle helped us raise a very important question: Who controls how capital is invested and why isn't it a more democratic process?

The World Bank Bond Boycott provides a local action—just about everyone has some connection to a church, college, union, or local government—and it connects this local action to global issues. Even if we don't quickly or directly impact the World Bank's ability to raise funds, the bond boycott is a good vehicle for educating the public about the many evils of the World Bank. Trying to pass a bond boycott resolution through a local institution also teaches valuable lessons about how we can get more control over the people's money.

Once you have picked an institution, you can present your

critique of why it should not own World Bank bonds. For useful information on the Bank, contact the 50 Years Is Enough Network (202-IMF-BANK) or check the website www.50years.org. For specific material on how to wage a World Bank bond boycott in your area contact the World Bank Bond Boycott office in Washington at (202) 299-0020 and visit the campaign's website at www.worldbankboycott.org.

Already there are city governments (Berkeley, Oakland, San Francisco), trade unions (Communications Workers of America, United Electrical, Radio and Machine Workers of America), and church groups (Sisters of Loretto, Illinois Disciples Foundation) that have passed bond boycott resolutions, and the campaign is spreading internationally (e.g., see the website of the European group A SEED, www.antenna.nl/aseed/mdb/mdb.htm).

What follows are a list of ways you can organize to support the World Bank Bond Boycott, and a sample resolution you can get passed by local institutions. We have reprinted the resolution passed by the Berkeley City Council. You can modify it to suit your local needs.

1. Hold a rally in solidarity with protests that occur each September and April at the IMF/World Bank meetings. Ideas for the rally:

Highlight your demand that your institution promise to not purchase World Bank bonds in the future.

Demonstrate in solidarity with a university in the Global South where students are fighting privatization or fee hikes.

Demonstrate at a local branch of Citibank (See #2)

2. Organize an action at a local Citibank. Demand that Citigroup's subsidiary Salomon Smith Barney no longer underwrite World Bank bonds. Contact Rainforest Action Network at www.ran.org for more on Citigroup's role in the Third World debt crisis, selling World Bank bonds, and other issues.

You can send a free fax to Salomon Smith Barney and you can get additional information from the website of the Transnational Research and Action Center (www.corpwatch.org).

3. Release a letter to your institution's treasurer, signed by community leaders, asking that your institution pledge not to purchase World Bank bonds in the future. A sample letter is available on the World Bank Bond Boycott website, www.worldbankboycott.org.

4. Form a local network of student and community groups to work on the World Bank bonds boycott in your city government and on your campus. Announce the formation of the network in a press conference. You can get advice from the 50 Years Is Enough office in Washington, D.C., (202) IMF-BANK.

5. Host a teach-in on corporate globalization. Invite a speaker to address the impacts of the IMF and World Bank, especially the effects of World Bank policies on education and students. Have a speaker who can help you strategize your participation in the World Bank bonds boycott. For speakers on this and related issues, contact either the boycott office, 50 Years Is Enough or Global Exchange (800) 497-1994.

Highlight the links between the struggles of working people in the U.S. with those in the Global South by inviting a member of a local struggle against privatization or for living wages.

6. Show a film about the IMF/World Bank and the growing movement against them, such as *Breaking the Bank, Deadly Embrace, Two Trevors Go to Washington, or Whose Globalization*? Then have a discussion and start a campaign to get your college or city government to boycott World Bank bonds. See www.worldbankboycott.org for how to get the videos.

7. Do street theater to dramatize global injustice in a prominent location on campus or downtown. Contact Alli Starr at Global Exchange (800) 497-1994, or United for a Fair Economy (www.ufenet.org), (617) 423-2148, for suggestions on skits and other resources on street theater.

8. Do a stickering and wheat-pasting with materials to raise awareness about the World Bank and the bonds boycott. We have creative, fun materials you can use. Send us an e-mail at bankboycott@econjustice.net to request a package of materials.

Sample Resolution Against Purchasing World Bank Bonds

WHEREAS, the World Bank controls more investment capital and, together with the International Monetary Fund, has more policy influence in the world economy than any other institution, and for the past fifty years the World Bank has accumulated more and more influence over the economic policies of less developed countries; and

WHEREAS, the World Bank uses its leverage over less developed countries to actively promote policies that favor the narrow profit interests of transnational corporations, such as low wages, proliferation of sweatshops, repressive labor policies, and weak environmental regulation, at the expense of the interests of the majority to improve living standards; and

WHEREAS, the World Bank imposes a narrowly defined, export-led growth model on Third World countries so they will earn more hard currency to make payments on foreign debts. To achieve this increase in exports, structural adjustment policies are imposed that include slashing public spending, jacking up interest rates to exorbitant levels, deregulating markets, devaluing currencies, and reducing existing labor protections. The impact on workers and their families is devastating. Workers face massive layoffs and wage cuts, while prices of basics such as food, housing, energy, and transportation skyrocket; and

WHEREAS, structural adjustment policies worsen U.S. trade deficits, leading to the loss of family-supporting jobs while driving down the already abysmally low wages of workers living in the developing nations. Requirements that Third World countries deregulate foreign investment pit poor countries and workers against each other in competition to attract foreign companies. This, in effect, leads to a race to the bottom in wages, working conditions, and environmental standards, as well as a loss of approximately one million U.S. jobs annually; and

WHEREAS, the World Bank's project lending is often environmentally destructive, and violates the rights of indigenous peoples; and

WHEREAS, the World Bank's policy that countries expand their exports has led poor countries to overexploit their natural resources by cutting down forests, heavily using chemicals to produce export crops, and overfishing coastal and international waters. The World Bank also funds controversial large-scale infrastructure projects that amount to millions of taxpayer dollars being wasted on corporate welfare; and

WHEREAS, by keeping the governments of low-income countries dependent on new infusions of capital from high-income countries, the World Bank has reinforced an external allegiance of these governments, making them more accountable to World Bank managers than to their own people; and with policy making in the hands of unelected bureaucrats, there is no real chance of either meaningful development or democracy taking place in many of these countries; and

WHEREAS, the World Bank operates in a secretive fashion and is accountable neither to the taxpayers who fund it nor to the citizens of debtor countries who are subjected to its policies;

THEREFORE be it resolved that, from this date forward, (*name of institution*) will not purchase bonds issued by the International Bank for Reconstruction and Development (the World Bank) or invest money in any investment fund that holds World Bank bonds.

It would be socially irresponsible to participate in supporting these policies and therefore Progressive Assets Management will not purchase bonds issued by the International Bank for Reconstruction and Development [World Bank].
Progressive Assets Management , 4/10/00

26

An Alternative to
the Debt Crisis?

Kevin Danaher

For many years we have known that one of the key impediments to development in the former colonial countries is that every year massive amounts of capital in the form of debt payments are transferred out of poor countries to banking institutions in the northern industrial countries.

A growing number of poor countries are unable to make payments on their foreign debt, or can only make the payments by cutting back on essential services for their people such as healthcare and education. This, added to growing pressure from human rights groups concerned about the suffering associated with the debt, have caused a growing number of people around the world to call for cancelling the debt of the poorest countries.

The problem with simple cancellation of the debt is that it gives a reprieve to third world elites—many of them undemocratic—without requiring any reforms. There is nothing to guarantee that they will use money freed up by debt relief to instead fund social services for the poor, and there is nothing to guarantee that they won't simply get their countries into debt all over again. In fact, being relieved from the pressure of debt payments could allow many third world elites to better resist local pressure for democratic change.

Attaching conditions to debt cancellation for third world *elites* is not necessarily a bad thing if majority forces in the global south control the process through which the conditionality is imposed. What if we could develop a global movement calling for "people's conditionality" that would shift capital and decision-making authority from the elites to the majority?

Here is one way it might work: Debtor governments would pay local currency into a local People's Development Commission (or whatever name local people choose). The government's only access to the account would be to make deposits, *not* to make withdrawals or influence expenditures—this would limit patronage problems. The Commission would have strict democratic requirements: It would be run by a board elected in free and fair elections with limits on campaign spending; the board would contain a large percentage of women; representation of workers and small farmers would be written into the charter; grassroots development organizations would figure prominently; and other requirements could be specified, all with the goal of ensuring democratic accountability and popular control of the capital. The precise details would need to be developed through a local, participatory process including diverse sectors of civil society, but the general principles—getting capital down to the grassroots and democratizing the process by which capital gets invested—would hold constant.

The People's Development Commission would use the money deposited into its account to issue loans and grants to grassroots development efforts. These could include a wide range of small-scale enterprises and empowerment projects: women's production and marketing cooperatives, organic farming projects, craft production, provision of health, education, transportation services, grassroots infrastructure development such as solar power, water purification, sanitation, and the list could go on. Putting a ceiling of a few thousand dollars on the size of grants and loans would tend to keep away the financial exploiters who usually are not interested in small amounts.

The Grameen Bank in Bangladesh and other micro-enterprise lenders provide useful lessons on how limits could be put on the size of loans, how the money could be paid back by collectives rather than individuals, and how the process could go beyond mere financial transactions to social organizing. The economic multiplier effect would be great because the poor spend most of their money in the local economy on basic things such as food, clothing, and shelter.

For each sum of local currency deposited into its People's Development Commission, the government of that nation would get their multilateral debt reduced for an equivalent amount of hard currency at a mutually agreed exchange rate. This would stop one of the biggest problems of the debt crisis: the bleeding of hard currency from debtor countries. Talk to people about the economic crisis on the streets of Zimbabwe, Nicaragua, or Haiti and eventually the discussion comes around to the problem of foreign exchange shortages.

This plan may be thought of as a *debt-for-democratic-development* swap. The problem with most debt-for-equity swaps is that they fail to transfer ownership to the local people. This plan would seek to ensure that money gets down to the base of societies, to be controlled by grassroots institutions.

The poor have proven that they can develop enterprise skills if they have access to capital. This plan would create some hope that development capital and decision-making power would get into the hands of the people who need it the most.

Another strength of this approach to debt cancellation is that it would require close collaboration between grassroots forces in the global south and north. Transnational majority forces would be coming together to devise ways to break up the functional unity of transnational elite alliances, thus satisfying the central dictum of all political struggle: Unite friends, divide adversaries.

Global Exchange is interested in getting your feedback on how this idea could be built into an international campaign led from the global south. Please send your comments and criticism to Kevin Danaher at Global Exchange, e-mail: kevin@globalexchange.org.

27

Twelve Ways to Democratize the U.S. Political System

Deborah James

The United States is the most powerful nation on the planet. Thus, U.S. residents have a special responsibility to democratize their own society, and in so doing, contribute to democratizing the global economy. Most Americans want a government that is truly of, by, and for the people, where community interests are prioritized above corporate interests.

We believe the following changes would move us in the direction of a more participatory democracy, in which people could influence policymaking regardless of the size of their bank accounts.

1. Demand full public funding of political campaigns at federal, state, and local levels.

In 1998, winning candidates in the Senate spent nearly twice as much as their opponents, and in House races three times as much. In 1996, 92 percent of House races and 88 percent of Senate races were won by the candidate who spent the most on the election. We need to rein in political contributions, especially unregulated soft money donations to parties. In 1996, the Democratic and Republican parties raised $260 million in soft money contributions. That number was expected to triple for the 2000 presidential election. We need a political system in which candidates who agree to forego private contributions and accept spending limits receive full public funds to run for office. We need comprehensive campaign finance reform that eliminates the need for fundraising, provides a financially level playing field for candidates, and closes loopholes. We should also promote a constitutional amendment acknowledging that money is not speech.

2. Abolish the electoral college.

The President is elected—*not* directly by voters—but by the Electoral College. Only 26 states require electors to follow the popular vote. Most state constitutions award electoral votes on a winner-take-all basis. For instance, if 48 percent of a state's voters vote for a Democrat and 47 percent vote for a Republican, and the state has six electoral votes, all six of that state's votes go to the Democratic candidate. Three times historically, the electoral college elected presidents who ran second in popular votes. This could happen again in a close race. The electoral college should be abolished to allow direct Presidential elections.

3. Promote third parties to create a multi-party democracy.

Both the Democratic and Republican parties support major corporate interests at the expense of the public. For real debate and democracy, we need more parties representing a broader range of interests. Many Americans abstain from voting because they are alienated by the two mainstream parties, whose candidates are pre-selected by wealthy contributors. We should make it easier for third parties to get on the ballot, participate in debates, get media coverage and receive public funding.

4. Promote ethics, disclosure, and information sharing.

Political appointees are far too often large campaign contributors, representing commercial interests rather than the public interest. The public needs complete, timely and accessible information about government appointments. We need stronger federal anti-bribery and gratuity statutes to ensure that special interests cannot use gifts to gain favor with public officials. Comprehensive and detailed financial disclosure by public officials is needed to help prevent conflicts of interest. We need to stop the revolving door between government and corporations.

5. Institute proportional representation and instant runoff procedures.

Our legislative elections are based on winner-take-all districts, meaning that the one candidate who gets a plurality of votes becomes the sole representative of that district. Minority viewpoints aren't represented in Congress or in state legislatures because new parties and perspectives are effectively shut out. With proportional representation, parties would receive seats in proportion to the percentage of votes received. All voters are represented—not just those voting for the winner. Small parties can win seats, so political debate becomes broader, new issues can be introduced more easily, and more people come out to vote. This system is used by most of the world's democracies and should be instituted in the United States. When voting for a single position, as in a presidential race, we should use the instant runoff system, in which voters rank candidates in order of preference. If your first choice does not receive a majority, your second choice is counted, and so on. This encourages people to vote for their preferred candidate without fear of "wasting" their vote.

6. Democratize media access.

Television and radio greatly influence the public's ideas about candidates and their positions. The candidates, in turn, require millions of dollars in contributions to buy political advertisements and reach the citizenry. The public has the right to hear all viewpoints regardless of the funds available to the candidates. Radio airwaves and television channels are public property. We must democratize access to the media by providing free or reduced-cost radio and television time to all candidates.

7. Educate citizens to participate in the democratic process.

An educated citizenry is an essential element of a true democracy. We need to realign national budgetary priorities to ensure that all citizens attain an educational level that would allow a true democracy to flourish. We need to provide civic education that encourages active participation in the democratic process beyond just voting, so that elected officials are accountable to the majority's interests rather than corporate interests.

8. Reduce wealth inequality.

Inequality in economic power distorts the democratic process. In a system where money controls politics, the concerns of poor people, particularly people of color, are not adequately addressed. People who are struggling to survive often do not have the time, education, or resources to fully participate in the political process. We need a national living wage so that all citizens have the opportunity to take part in our democracy.

9. End discrimination in the criminal justice system.

Discrimination in the criminal justice system distorts democracy. As our judicial system continues to arrest, prosecute, and convict people of color at disproportionately higher rates than whites, and incarcerated people are barred from exercising their right to vote, communities of color are further marginalized. Twelve states ban former prisoners from voting, for life. No other country in the world permanently disenfranchises ex-offenders. Close to four million Americans are now excluded from the political process, including roughly 13 percent of the country's African American men. We need to repeal laws that disenfranchise former prisoners to allow them to have a stake in the democratic process.

10. Institute voting and citizenship rights for immigrants.

Citizenship and voting constitute the most fundamental rights of our society, and no one who lives here permanently should be denied those rights. The Constitution gives states the right to determine the qualifications for voting. In the nineteenth century some states granted non-citizen immigrants the right to vote in elections. Immigrants should have the right to vote or to become citizens within one year. The U.S. should also join other countries in recognizing dual citizenship in order to make it easier for immigrants to participate in our society without having to repudiate their homeland.

11. Make voting easy.

Politicians tell us that the United States is the world's leading democracy, but most countries have higher rates of voter turnout. Only 38 percent of eligible voters participated in the 1998 elections—and only 17.4 percent voted in the 1998 primaries. Apathy and cynicism increasingly threaten our democracy. Voter apathy is caused by a combination of factors, including corporate control of politics through campaign contributions, lack of diversity in parties and candidates, and logistical hurdles to voting. Voter registration should be easy, available until the day before an election, and automatic every time we move. We should have voter identification cards—not driver's licenses—as our primary means of citizen identification. Voter registration drives should reach out to register people in communities of color and poor communities who have been traditionally marginalized from the electoral process. Election day should be a national holiday, or on the weekend.

12. Ensure freedom of political expression.

People should have the right to express their political opinions without fear of state repression. Police officers should work to ensure that our First Amendment rights to freedom of speech, including political protest, are guaranteed. Police should be prevented from harassing, intimidating, or using violence against peaceful protesters.

Conclusion

Perhaps the most promising aspect of the movement for global justice is that more and more individuals and organizations are asking questions about how capital gets invested. At the level of global rule-making, protesters are demanding fundamental changes in the way the WTO, the IMF, and the World Bank favor corporate profit-making instead of prioritizing the neeeds of people and the planet. Corporate accountability campaigners are pressuring companies to shift their policies toward social and environmental sustainability. Social entrepreneurs are creating alternative systems of finance, production, and distribution through socially responsible investing, renewable energy systems, community supported agriculture, local currencies, micro-enterprise lending, fair trade practices, eco-labelling, and many other alternative economic institutions.

How capital gets invested affects our jobs, our standard of living, the environment, gender inequality, race relations, housing, healthcare, transportation, immigration, our culture, and just about everything else in our lives.

Within the global movement for changing how capital gets invested, there are two key questions being asked: Who is sitting at the table when the investment decisions get made?; and what are the values guiding the process? If the people sitting at the table are a monocrop (wealthy, white males) then the policies coming from that decision-making process cannot reflect the needs and desires of the rest of us. Think of how a monocrop works: All other forms of life must be suppressed. So a monocrop of pro-corporate voices at the decision-making table will shut out other sectors of society such as workers, environmentalists, churches, community groups, and others. Thus "democracy" becomes an empty phrase because the diversity of voices that is essential for real democracy is blocked by those with power not wanting to share it.

The second question being posed regarding how capital gets invested is: What values guide the process? The free market ideology that has dominated public discourse in recent decades—but is now increasingly challenged—requires that social voices other than commerce be shut out of the policy debate: The love of life must be silenced so the love of money can hold sway. Greed replaces both compassion and environmental sensitivity as the core value of society. The dominant criterion is to maximize the profits of private corporations by turning nature and human labor into marketable commodities, thus ensuring that the bioshphere will be destroyed and human rights will get trampled.

There is now a mass movement demanding new values for the capital investment process: Meet all social needs (of all people) and save the environment. These radically different values are being manifested in many ways: socially responsible investing, consumer pressure campaigns, shareholder resolutions insisting on different types of corporate accountability, the anti-sweatshop movement, and many others. The idea of social accountability and environmental protection is so widely accepted that the power brokers can no longer turn a blind eye. Witness the World Bank now claiming that its central goal is to end poverty, and oil corporations insisting that they care about preserving the environment.

A growing percentage of the activists attacking the World Bank, IMF, and WTO understand that these institutions are fronting for corporate capitalism. So more and more of the movement's work is focused on ending corporate rule in all its forms—not just the Bretton Woods institutions.

The wall protecting the free market ideology is cracking. Large sections of the public are increasingly critical of corporate rule and its consequences. As a September 11, 2000 cover story in *Business Week* ("Too Much Corporate Power?") revealed, 74 percent of the public say big corporations have too much power, and 73 percent say top executives get paid too much. Only four percent of those interviewed agreed with the statement, "U.S. corporations should have only one purpose—to make the most profit for their shareholders—and their pursuit of that goal will be best for America in the long run." But 95 percent of those polled agreed with the following statement: "U.S. corporations should have more than one purpose. They also owe something to their workers and the communities in which they operate, and they should sometimes sacrifice some profit for the sake of making things better for their workers and communities."[1]

There are many signs of hope not reported by the corporate media. For example, trade unions are rebounding from their decades-long slump and are increasing in size and sophistication. Especially encouraging are two trends in the global trade union movement. (1) More and more unions are going beyond focusing solely on the needs of their members to build broader alliances with nongovernmental groups struggling for social justice and saving the environment. (2) Unions are also gradually moving beyond nationalist politics to realize that, if capital is transnational, then workers must also organize transnationally to be effective.

Grassroots organizations in all sectors—environmental, human rights, church-based, youth, and women's groups—are organizing transnationally. This grassroots internationalism has reached such proportions that it now challenges the elite, corporate version of globalization.

The Two Globalizations

The mass media talk about globalization as if it were a unified, all-encompassing entity. But there are two kinds of globalization: elite globalization and grassroots globalization.

The top-down globalization promoted by the big corporations is characterized by a constant drive to maximize profits. It forces countries to open up to large corporations, reduce and privatize state functions, deregulate the economy, be "efficient" and competitive, submit everything and everyone to the rule of "market forces." In practice, economic production is increasingly disconnected from human needs; people are encouraged to pursue an unsustainable pattern of resource consumption; and social inequality has reached grotesque levels. The United Nations Development Program reports that the richest 20 percent of the world's people account for 86 percent of global consumption spending and the poorest 80 percent of the world's population accounts for just 14 percent of consumption spending.

In the face of this predatory type of globalization, there is another kind of globalization being forged; a globalization that reaffirms the primacy of the ethical principles that form the foundation of true democracy: equality, freedom, participation, human diversity, and solidarity. This grassroots variant of globalization is made up of many large movements: the fair trade movement, micro-lending networks, the movement for social and ecological labeling, sister cities and sister schools, trade union solidarity across borders, and many others. While these constituents of grassroots globalization lack the money and government influence possessed by the corporations, they showed at the World Trade Organization protests in Seattle in late 1999 that they are capable of mobilizing enough people to halt the corporate agenda in its tracks—at least, temporarily.

Yet we must do more than denounce and disrupt corporate rule. We must do more than make individual corporations more socially responsible (e.g., by adopting green labeling practices) or more publicly accountable (e.g., public disclosure of information on investments and operations). Most groups working to democratize the economy favor a particular tactic (e.g., boycotts, shareholder resolutions, demonstrations), or they focus on a particular corporation or industry, or they are limited to a particular country or region. They often fail to take on the systemic issues of corporate power. Most of these struggles could be characterized as "end-of-pipeline" struggles: They are reacting to the way corporate policies impact on people and the environment, rather than putting corporations on the defensive by questioning their right to dominate society the way they do. Even successful corporate accountability struggles do not usually threaten the existence of the corporation.

This is the critique voiced by the Program on Corporations, Law and Democracy (POCLAD), a group that questions the efficacy of struggles to change a particular corporate policy. "We all know stories about small, low-budget groups stopping global corporations from siting a deadly factory, clear-cutting a forest, ram-rodding through a new law, busting a union, using deceptive advertising, carrying propaganda into a school," says POCLAD director Richard Grossman. "But have you wondered why, despite all this good activist work, corporate assaults against life and democracy keep increasing? When the joy of victory fades, imperial corporations remain. Slowed down in one place, they pop up in another. They keep blocking sane, logical transitions in food, energy, transportation, health care, finance, forestry, and manufacturing. They keep funding think tanks and university corporations to frame public debate. Radio, television, magazine, and movie corporations keep selling their relentless message: 'Corporations: efficient, good. Government: wasteful, bad.'"

POCLAD calls for people to:

• challenge judicial doctrines asserting that the corporation is a legal person and has property rights in decision making;

• build campaigns to get state attorneys general to revoke the charters of companies that violate the public interest;

• amend state corporation codes to end limited liability and to ban corporations from owning other corporations; and

• exclude corporations and their trade associations from involvement in elections, lawmaking, and education.

Author Jim Hightower advocates a seven-word amendment to the U.S. Constitution that would read: "A corporation is not a human being." It would be difficult for our opponents to argue that a corporation *is* a human being, and if the amendment passed it would pull the legal rug out from under the political power of corporations.

The Native American organization Seventh Generation calls for an amendment to the U.S. Constitution stating: "The right of citizens of the U.S. to enjoy and use air, water, sunlight, and other renewable resources determined by the Congress to be common property shall not be impaired, nor shall such use impair their availability for use by future generations." It only takes a moment of serious thinking to see how the normal operations of corporate America would be called into question by such a legally enforceable definition of sustainability.

Whether or not progressive forces take up the larger strategy of questioning the legal status of corporations, there is a growing consensus within the movement that we must evolve from disparate, piecemeal approaches to a more systemic focus that seeks to change the basic rules of the game.

The Road Ahead

In the 21st century, our task is to build a worldwide movement for democratic control over our economic and environmental future. This "globalization from below" will build the institutional foundation for a participatory and sustainable global society. To accomplish such a huge task requires that we get more professional about the art and science of practicing democracy. We don't mean "democracy" in the current sense of occasionally entering a voting booth to choose from a narrow range of candidates selected by a process most of us don't understand. Rather, we are building a *participatory* democracy in which the citizens redefine politics so they can embrace it and practice it as avidly as they now participate in sports or shopping.

Corporate accountability organizations have made great advances in the art and science of popular democracy. They have educated and mobilized the public on issues ranging from environmental justice to labor rights to genetic engineering. They have forced government at all levels to make changes in policy that were not in the interest of the dominant elites. They have established codes of conduct for corporate behavior. They have changed popular tastes and shifted the terms of debate on smoking, forest destruction, junk food, biotechnology, and large questions such as whether or not we should trust corporations to operate in the public interest.

Beyond any specific changes achieved by corporate accountability groups, they are also helping to create a "we" ideology in place of the dominant "me" ideology of corporate consumer culture. Individual organizations are learning how to subordinate their institutional egos to the larger needs of the movement. Organizations in the global north are learning how to take direction from partners in the global south. We are creating organizational structures that are truly transnational. Organizing efforts such as the WTO protests in Seattle, the IMF/World Bank protests in Washington, and the World Social Forum in Brazil in January 2001 are building the foundation for global political structures "of, by, and for the people" rather than of, by, and for the corporations.

More and more people are beginning to break through the cult of powerlessness and now believe that we can build a truly democratic global economy. But the pressing question is: Can we achieve that goal soon enough to prevent the biosphere and millions of people from being destroyed by the built-in rapaciousness of global capitalism?

The answer will be determined, in part, by what you do after you put down this book.

Footnotes
1. Special report by Aaron Bernstein, "Too Much Corporate Power?" *Business Week*, September 11, 2000.

Resources

Organizations

Because of the size and diversity of the movement for democratizing the global economy we cannot list all the groups involved. Below are some of the groups we have worked with most closely. Our apologies to those left out.

Global Exchange, (800) 497-1994, www.globalexchange.org

50 Years is Enough, (202) IMF-BANK (463-2265) www.50years.org Check out their tool kit, "Unpacking Globalization" for excellent educational resources.

Alliance for Democracy, (781) 894-1179, www.afd-online.org

Campaign for Labor Rights, (202) 544-9355, www.summersault.com/~agj/clr/

Essential Action, (202) 387-8030 www.essential.org

Fairness and Accuracy in Reporting, (800) 847-3993, www.fair.org.

Focus on the Global South, Bangkok, Thailand, 66-2-2187363, www.focusweb.org

Independent Media Center, (888) 686-9252, www.indymedia.org

Institute for Agriculture and Trade Policy, (612) 870-0453, www.iatp.org

Institute for Policy Studies, (202) 234-9382, www.ips-dc.org

International Forum on Globalization, (415) 229-9350, www.ifg.org

Jobs with Justice, (202) 434-1106, www.jwj.org

JustAct, (415) 431-4204, www.justact.org

Program on Corporations, Law and Democracy, (800) 316-2739 www.poclad.org

Public Citizen's Global Trade Watch/Citizens Trade Campaign (202) 546-4996, www.tradewatch.org

Student Alliance to Reform Corporations, www.corpreform.org

Third World Network, (Malaysia) www.twnside.org.sg

Tobin Tax Initiative, (707) 822-8347, www.ceedweb.org/iirp/

TransFair USA, (510) 663-5260, www.transfairusa.org

Transnational Research and Action Center, (415) 561-6568, www.corpwatch.org

United Students Against Sweatshops, www.umich.edu/~sole/usas

Women's EDGE: Economic Development and Global Equality, (202) 884-8396, www.womensedge.org

Women's Environment and Development Organization, (212) 973-0325, www.wedo.org

World Bank Bond Boycott Campaign, (202) 299-0020, www.worldbankboycott.org

Recommended Publications

Books

The Cancer Stage of Capitalism, John McMurtry (London: Pluto Press, 1999).

Localization: A Global Manifesto, Colin Hines (London: Earthscan, 2000).

Globalization and the Decline of Social Reform, Gary Teeple (New Jersey: Humanities Press, 1995).

The Cult of Impotence: Selling the Myth of Powerlessness in the Global Economy, Linda McQuaig (New York: Viking, 1998).

Good Taxes: The Case for Taxing Foreign Currency Exchange and Other Financial Transactions, Alex C. Michalos (Toronto: Dundurn Press, 1997).

Taming Global Finance: A Better Architecture for Growth and Equity, Robert A. Blecker (Washington, D.C.: Economic Policy Institute, 1999).

Globalization from Below: The Power of Solidarity, Jeremy Brecher, et al., (Cambridge, MA: South End Press, 2000).

Masters of Illusion: The World Bank and the Poverty of Nations, Catherine Caufield (New York: Henry Holt and Co., 1996).

Periodicals

ColorLines: Race/Culture/Action, (510) 653-3415, www.colorlines.com

Corporate Crime Reporter, (202) 737-1680

Multinational Monitor, (202) 234-5176, www.essential.org/monitor/

The Progressive Populist, (800) 732-4992, www.populist.com

Yes: A Journal of Positive Futures, (206) 842-0216, www.futurenet.org

Resources Available from Global Exchange

Globalize This!: The Battle Against the World Trade Organization and Corporate Rule, ed. by Kevin Danaher and Roger Burbach (Monroe, ME, Common Courage Press, 2000). The

WTO threatens diversity, labor rights, the environment, and even democracy itself in their push for elite globalization. Kevin Danaher's latest release shows why these institutions must be stopped and how to go about it. (224 pp., $15.95)

50 Years is Enough: The Case Against the World Bank and the International Monetary Fund, ed. by Kevin Danaher (Boston: South End Press, 1994). Thirty-six chapters cover all the bases: international context, country case studies, women, the environment, tribal peoples, and alternatives. Includes a resources section and guide to organizations. (210 pp., $16)

Corporations Are Gonna Get Your Mama: Globalization and the Downsizing of the American Dream, ed. by Kevin Danaher (Monroe, ME: Common Courage Press, 1996). Two dozen noted authors explain how corporate globalization is undermining democracy and the standard of living in America. (224 pp., $15.95)

Globalization in Our Own Front Yard. This easy-to-understand pamphlet connects the structural adjustment policies that have ravaged the third world and the ongoing destruction of the social safety net here in the U.S. (24 pp., $2)

Voices from the WTO: An Anthology of Writings by the People Who Shutdown the World Trade Organization in Seattle. Students, steelworkers, farmers, teachers, teamsters, peace activists, and others, document why they joined forces against the WTO. (96 pp., $10)

Call or write for a complete list or visit us on-line at: www.globalexchange.org/store.

Videos

Whose Globalization?—These two half hour talks by Global Exchange cofounder Kevin Danaher will give you a clear contrast between the elite globalization promoted by the World Bank/IMF and the grassroots globalization of the global justice movement. (65 minutes, $25)

Breaking the Bank—A must for anyone wanting to learn more about the protests against the IMF and the World Bank. The film balances dramatic scenes from the streets of DC with analytical segments on IMF/World Bank policies. Produced in conjunction with the Independent Media Center. (72 minutes, $25)

Showdown in Seattle: Five Days that shook the WTO—This five-part series gives on-the-ground and in-depth analysis of world trade issues and popular resistance. Each half-hour show is made up of segments shot and edited during the WTO protests by video producers from around the U.S. working with the Independent Media Center. (137 minutes, $25)

Santiago's Story—Caught in a system of exploitation, most coffee farmers never earn enough from their harvest to rise out of poverty. This video tells the story of coffee grower Santiago Rivera, who joined a Fair Trade farmers' cooperative in search of a living wage. (16 minutes, $15)

Sweating for a T-Shirt—Shows how workers making clothes for U.S. colleges earn $3.50/day when the basic cost of living is $8/day. Hear sweatshop workers tell about long hours, sicknesses from the workplace, and harassment trying to form unions. Follow workers to see their living conditions. In English or Spanish. (23 minutes, $25.)

Audio Cassettes

Global Exchange offers dozens of informative audio tapes examining crucial international issues. Produced by David Barsamian's Alternative Radio, these programs can be enjoyed in the comfort of your car or home. The list of many speakers includes: Howard Zinn, Cornel West, Noam Chomsky, Ralph Nader, Lani Guinier, Angela Davis, Vandana Shiva, and GX's Kevin Danaher. They average 60 minutes in length. For a complete list of our cassette selection call us at 1-800-497-1994 or go on-line to www.globalexchange.org/store. The tapes are $10 each, postpaid ($20 for double cassettes).

Contributors

Michael Albert is a co-founder of South End Press, an editor of *Z Magazine,* and is a principal writer with ZNET, a progressive internet news and analysis service.

Terry J. Allen reports for *In These Times.*

Soren Ambrose is a senior analyst with the 50 Years Is Enough Network in Washington, D.C.

Juliette Beck is program coordinator for the Global Democracy Project at Global Exchange.

Walden Bello is Director of Focus on the Global South in Bangkok, Thailand.

Patrick Bond is a professor in the Graduate School of Public and Development Management, University of the Witwatersrand, South Africa.

Nicola Bullard is a policy anaylst with Focus on the Global South in Bangkok, Thailand.

Madeleine Bunting is Religious Affairs Editor for *The Guardian* in London.

George Caffentzis is profeessor of Philosophy at the University of Southern Maine in Portland, and he is active with the Committee for Academic Freedom in Africa (CAFA).

Fidel Castro is the President of Cuba.

Noam Chomsky is a noted author and professor of Linguistics at Massachusetts Institute of Technology.

Rachel Coen is Communications Coordinator for FAIR, Fairness and Accuracy in Reporting, the media watchdog group based in New York.

Charlie Cray is Associate Editor of *Multinational Monitor* in Washington, D.C.

Kevin Danaher is a co-founder of Global Exchange and editor of *Corporations Are Gonna Get Your Mama: Globalization and the Downsizing of the American Dream*, and co-editor with Roger Burbach of *Globalize This!: The Battle Against the World Trade Organization and Corporate Rule*.

Silvia Federici is professor of Political Philosophy at Hofstra University and she is active with the Committee for Academic Freedom in Africa (CAFA).

Korinna Horta is Senior Economist at Environmental Defense and a contributing writer to *Multinational Monitor*.

Deborah James is the Director of the Fair Trade Program at Global Exchange.

Naomi Klein is author of *No Logo: Taking Aim at the Brand Bullies* (New York: St. Martin's Press, 1999).

Anuradha Mittal is Co-Director of Food First, the Institute for Food and Development Policy in Oakland, California.

David Moberg is a Senior Editor at *In These Times* and a Fellow of the Nation Institute.

Njoki Njoroge Njehu is the Director of the 50 Years Is Enough Network based in Washington, D.C.

Margot Smith is a writer and activist living in Berkeley, CA.

Starhawk is an author, nonviolence trainer and practitioner of the arts of magical activism. She has written many books, the most recent of which is *Walking to Mercury*.

Alli Starr is a co-founder of Art and Revolution and is currently an all-around hellraiser at Global Exchange.

Tamara Straus writes for the electronic news service, AlterNet.

Neil Watkins is Director of the World Bank Bonds Boycott campaign based in Washington, D.C.

Robert Weissman is the Editor of *Multinational Monitor* in Washington, D.C.

Index

GLOBAL ⊙ EXCHANGE

Global Exchange is an international human rights organization dedicated to promoting justice around the world. Since our founding in 1988, we have worked to increase global awareness by the U.S. public while building international partnerships around the world.

Political and Civil Rights Campaigns: Global Exchange complements the traditional human rights organizations' observation and monitoring work with activities aimed at directly empowering the grassroots human rights and pro-democracy movements within target countries and building support for these movements in the United States. We also work to improve relations between the U.S. and countries with whom we have been in conflict.

Economic Rights: Global Exchange monitors corporate behavior and that of the global rule-makers such as the World Bank, the IMF, and the World Trade Organization, taking action to ensure workers are treated fairly and that labor and environmental rights are at the core of international trade and finance deliberations.

Reality Tours: Our educational tours take travelers beyond the isolation of resorts and cultural stereotypes by arranging meetings with grassroots organizations and community leaders in countries such as Cuba, Mexico, Haiti, Northern Ireland, South Africa, India, Israel/Palestine, and Brazil.

Exploring California: Our tours in the largest U.S. state give diverse people a chance to engage in solution-oriented dialogue on issues such as immigration, the treatment of laborers, and the environment by taking them to meet and speak with people involved in the issues. Exploring California also invites participants to support the innovative civic groups working to improve California.

Public Education: Global Exchange produces books, videos, articles and editorials; organizes educational events and workshops; and works with the media to increase coverage of international issues from a grassroots perspective. Our Speakers Bureau brings human rights leaders from other countries to the U.S. to share their stories with the public.

Fair Trade: Our two Fair Trade stores and our on-line store (www.globalexchange.org/store) generate income for artisans and farmers in 40 countries and give consumers a "sweat-free" alternative. Fair Trade gives ordinary people here in the U.S. an easy, everyday way to help build economic justice from the bottom up.

See the next page for how you can get involved in Global Exchange's programs.

Global Exchange works to create more justice and economic opportunity in the world. The heart of our work is the involvement of thousands of supporters around the country.

When you become a member of Global Exchange you get:

- our quarterly newsletter and Action Alerts;
- priority on our Reality Tours to dozens of foreign countries and domestic destinations;
- a 10 percent discount on our educational materials and the crafts we sell at our third world craft stores;
- regular updates on our human rights campaigns and our support for development projects.

Plus, you get connected to a growing international network of concerned citizens working to transform the world from the bottom up.

Please use the coupon below or our toll-free number (800) 497-1994 to join Global Exchange today.

- -

YES, I support Global Exchange's efforts to reform the global economy. Here is my tax-deductible membership donation:

___ $100   ___ $50   ___ $35

Name_____

Address_____

City_____State_____Zip_____

Phone_____ Email_____

GLOBAL EXCHANGE

2017 Mission Street, Suite 303, San Francisco, CA 94110
(415) 255-7296, FAX (415) 255-7498
email: info@globalexchange.org
website: www.globalexchange.org

Also Available from
Global Exchange and Common Courage Press

Globalize This!
The Battle Against the World Trade Organization and Corporate Rule
edited by
Kevin Danaher and Roger Burbach

Twenty-six chapters explain what happened at the WTO protests in Seattle, what's wrong with the WTO, and what the movement for global justice is proposing as an alternative. Chapters include: Paul Hawken, "Skeleton Woman Visits Seattle"; Elizabeth Martinez, "Where Was the Color in Seattle?"; Starhawk, "How We Really Shut Down the WTO"; Walden Bello, "Reforming the WTO Is the Wrong Agenda"; Susan George, "Fixing or Nixing the WTO"; Martin Khor, "Seattle Debacle: Revolt of the Developing Nations"; Medea Benjamin, "The Debate Over Tactics"; Manning Marable, "Seattle and Beyond"; Vandana Shiva, "Spinning a New Mythology: The WTO as Protector of the Poor"; Peter Rosset, "A New Food Movement Comes of Age in Seattle"; William Greider, "It's Time to Go On the Offensive: Here's How"; Robin Round, "Time for a Tobin Tax"; Tony Clarke, "Rewriting the Rules for Global Investment"; Deborah James, "Fair Trade, Not Free Trade"; and many more. (220 pages, $15.95)

Available on-line at www.commoncouragepress.org, or www.globalexchange.org/store or call (800) 497-1994.